The Revival of Resistance
The 2022-3 strikes, and the battles still to come

Mark L Thomas, Jessica Walsh and Charlie Kimber

The Revival of Resistance: The 2022-3 strikes, and the battles still to come
Mark L Thomas, Jessica Walsh and Charlie Kimber

Published 2023 by Bookmarks Publications
c/o 1 Bloomsbury Street, London WC1B 3QE
© Bookmarks Publications

Typeset by Simon Assaf
Design by Peter Robinson
Cover design: Yuri Prasad
Cover image: Guy Smallman
Printed by Halstan Limited

ISBN 978-1-914143-70-0 (pbk)

Introduction	5
Chapter 1: The strike movement 2022-3 – a balance sheet	8
Chapter 2: What is the trade union bureaucracy?	24
Chapter 3: A brief history of rank-and-file organisation	33
Chapter 4: The resistance that shook France	43
Chapter 5: Politics, trade unions and strikes	57
An Activist's Guide to Strikes and Trade Unions	67

Introduction

The strikes that began in Britain in the summer of 2022 marked a long overdue revival of working-class resistance.

After a long drought of strikes, when annual government reports on the state of the trade unions boasted of "historic lows" in the number of strikes in the preceding year, something important has changed.

Simmering resentment at the opulence of the rich, bullying by bosses, soaring company profits, hollow praise for workers' sacrifices and suffering during the pandemic, and a huge squeeze on pay packets as prices spiralled upwards, found a focus when workers voted to strike and hit the picket lines.

By early 2023, the number of strike days taken by workers since June 2022 was already higher than for any year since 1989.

This rediscovery by significant numbers of workers of their ability to take collective action is something to be celebrated. And for many it was their first time on strike.

But the aim of this short book is to do more than just celebrate the new strike movement.

The experience of the last year has also thrown into relief some of the barriers that need to be overcome if the strikes are to deepen and develop further.

Some of these obstacles are, of course, the arsenal of responses from employers, government and the corporate media. They include the restrictions of the anti-union laws, the anti-strike propaganda pumped out on TV and radio and in newspapers, the hostile treatment of trade unionists in interviews, the bullying and intimidation from employers and so on.

But a central argument of this book is that serious difficulties to expanding workers' capacity to fight against these external challenges lie within the workers' movement, and in particular the union leaderships and the wider trade union bureaucracy of paid officials.

The book puts forward an initial assessment of the strike movement, a balance sheet of gains and weaknesses and outlines an understanding of why the trade union bureaucracy behaves in ways that are often at odds with the interests of the union members they claim to represent.

It also points to movements from the past when groups of workers have found a way to challenge and overcome the constraints on struggle imposed by the union bureaucracy – rank-and-file organisation.

While workers in Britain have been rediscovering the strike weapon on a significant scale, 2023 was also marked by an even more intense level of struggle on the other side of the English Channel in France. We provide a survey of that revolt and again seek to draw out the key question of the role of the union leaders and union bureaucracy, an issue not swept away by the much higher level of resistance undertaken by workers in France since January 2023.

The final chapter looks at the role of politics in strikes and the trade unions. It challenges the notion that strikes are simply "economic" issues while politics should be left to the Labour Party. It puts forward the case for the unity of politics and economics that is central to rebuilding working-class struggle and organisation.

The strikes have brought into struggle a new generation of strikers and a new layer of young people have supported and visited picket lines, discussing with strikers the way forward for their disputes. This has raised many general questions about strikes, the unions and the working-class movement.

In November 2022, *Socialist Worker* published a very useful "Activists' Guide to Strikes and Trade Unions" tackling many of the questions that have arisen. We have included this at the end of the book.

The book is written by three members of the Socialist Workers Party, a revolutionary socialist organisation, that is committed to Karl Marx's famous injunction that workers' emancipation, their freedom, must be the act of workers themselves, won through their own struggles.

Strikes are a vital step in this process, but to develop their full potential requires a sharp challenge to the union bureaucracy, the growth of rank-and-file organisation and the development of a revolutionary party deeply rooted in the working class. We present this book as a small contribution to this task.

Authors

Mark L Thomas is a Trade Union and Workplace Organiser for the Socialist Workers Party

Jessica Walsh is a Trade Union and Workplace Organiser for the Socialist Workers Party

Charlie Kimber is the editor of *Socialist Worker*, the Socialist Workers Party's weekly newspaper

Chapter 1: The strike movement 2022-3 – a balance sheet

"This strike will spur a movement. We're standing up for the whole movement. Everyone's in the same boat, we're all feeling the pinch. We're all having to pay high prices for petrol and food. I hope this is a worthwhile movement for others to look at and say, 'If the RMT can do it, so can I'." **RMT striker, June 2022**

"I do think there's a real feeling at the moment, and it wouldn't surprise me if there was some kind of general strike. You pick up the paper or read the news, and there's another group of workers going out. Train drivers, barristers, there are so many different sectors. The more people you get together collectively, it sends out a more powerful message… You've got to stick together." **A Royal Mail striker, September 2022**

"We had over 300 people that stopped working. We only planned to strike two hours before it actually happened. When we did, the managers said we wouldn't get paid unless we returned to work. But everyone stayed and we didn't go back." **Amazon worker in Coventry after the summer's wildcat strikes**

"I think more people need to come out on strike if they can't afford to live – especially in the health service. Everyone should mobilise, from ambulance workers to cleaners. Everyone should strike."
A nurse educator in the Royal College of Nursing

"We had a ballot and voted in big numbers for a strike. It was bubbling in the garage: a really hectic mood. People thought, 'Let's stick it to them'. Arriva panicked. Management knew they were going into a fight they weren't going to easily win." **An Arriva bus driver in London**

"They're all out. There must be a couple of hundred dockers picketing today and they've got all the gates covered. The mood is fantastic. They're really happy to be out – really confident."
Socialist Worker **report of the Liverpool dockers' strike**

"Between June 2022 and February 2023 there have been increasing numbers of strikes occurring across a range of industries, including many parts of the rail and bus networks, postal workers, civil servants, teaching staff and the NHS… Recent labour disputes have occurred in the wider context of the UK's rising cost of living."
Office for National Statistics, March 2023

Summer 2022: a new hope

Over the summer of 2022, workers in Britain began to fight back on a scale not seen for a generation. Nationwide RMT (National Union of Rail, Maritime and Transport Workers) strikes at Network Rail and over a dozen train companies across Britain's privatised rail industry began in late June. They were followed over the summer by telecoms workers at BT Openreach, postal workers across Royal Mail and train drivers in Aslef (Associated Society of Locomotive Engineers and Firemen). An unprecedented strike by criminal barristers saw the growing strike movement spread to professional workers, many without any previous experience of collective militancy.

Over the autumn and winter of 2022-3, the strikes expanded to encompass UCU (University and College Union) and Unison members in the universities and PCS (Public and Commercial Services Union) members in the civil service. In the weeks before Christmas, tens of thousands of ambulance workers, nurses and other health workers also began strike action, as did tens of thousands of teachers in Scotland. In February, across England and Wales, over a quarter of a million members of the National Education Union (NEU) joined them.

As each new group of workers entered the fight, the enthusiasm was palpable. There had been no all-grades national rail strike since 1993, nor a national strike in BT since 1987. The Royal College of Nursing

(RCN) had never been on strike in England and Wales in its 106-year history! Rail workers' picket lines became a focus for wider solidarity, with local socialists helping turn many into rallies or local marches. The postal workers' picket lines were big and vibrant, and both the PCS and NEU reported unprecedented numbers of picket lines, often with the participation of large numbers of younger workers striking for the first time. Everywhere there was a sense of being part of a wider revolt, and the phrase "we should all strike together" was a constant refrain.

The enthusiasm saw a surge of new members in unions that were balloting and striking. Most dramatically, the NEU gained 50,000 new members in the weeks after it announced strike days.

Alongside the national strikes, mainly in the public sector or recently privatised industries, there was a pattern of smaller scale, but powerful strikes in private industry, again often marked by big picket lines. These were concentrated in certain sectors: refuse workers, bus drivers, logistics and transport, and at two major docks, Felixstowe, the busiest port in Britain, and Liverpool, neither of which had seen strikes for a quarter of a century or more. There was also a flurry of disputes at airports, often winning concessions with just the threat of action.

All of the above were "official" disputes, that is, organised with the backing and sanction of national trade unions through the legally imposed (and time consuming) process of postal ballots which, since 2016, have had to meet a minimum turnout threshold of 50 percent. Indeed, a significant development was that for the first time both the UCU in the universities and the NEU in England and Wales broke through this barrier in a single national ballot.

But there was also a smaller revival of "unofficial" action. In Amazon, where aside from handfuls of individual union members there was no union to organise an official ballot, walkouts nevertheless spread across a number of its massive warehouses over a week in August 2022. A strike like this by non-unionised workers had not been seen for decades. By early 2023, one of the larger general unions, the GMB (General Municipal and Boilermakers' Union), had recruited widely enough to successfully ballot and call strikes at Amazon's Coventry hub.

In the North Sea, workers on the oil and gas rigs were unionised but, coming together as a network of rank-and-file activists, they were able to launch strikes in defiance of the official union structures which were deemed too unresponsive and too enmeshed in partnership arrangements with employers. And in construction, longer standing networks of rank-and-file activists were able to organise unofficial walkouts over pay demands.

There were also examples of solidarity strikes. When ships were re-routed away from the striking Liverpool docks to Southampton, dockers there refused to unload them. Such "secondary action", once a widespread and powerful workers' weapon, was made unlawful in the early 1990s. But it seems bosses took no legal action against the Southampton dockers or their union Unite, perhaps fearful that it would provoke more walkouts. And in schools there were many reports of support staff in England, after narrowly failing to hit the turnout threshold in their own ballots, refusing to cross teachers' picket lines.

The cumulative impact of all this was notable. Between June 2022 and January 2023, the number of strike days recorded by the government stood at 2.691 million, with 843,000 in December alone. This was the highest since 1989 – when Margaret Thatcher was still in office!

When Mick Lynch, the RMT leader, who shot to popular celebrity for his pugnacious defences of the rail strikes in the media, proclaimed that "the working class is back", it caught the feeling of hundreds of thousands of activists in the working-class movement.

For decades the idea of workers' militancy seemed little more than a half-remembered story from an ever more distant past. A set of "common sense" arguments, held widely on the left and among trade union activists themselves, suggested that a major revival of strikes faced near impossible hurdles due to structural changes in the makeup of the working class.

The decline of employment in the old industries such as mining, shipbuilding and manufacturing, once the backbone of Britain's working-class movement, was assumed to mean the contemporary workforce, increasingly concentrated in service sector or white collar jobs, lacked the power to challenge employers in the way their predecessors had (and that the smaller numbers still employed in manufacturing had also been stripped of their former power).

Alongside this went the misplaced, but widely accepted, notion that "precarious", insecure, work was now so universal as to make collective action near impossible. And a third argument proclaimed that former collectivist ideas and traditions had been destroyed, with workers' ideas successfully reshaped by the assaults on the unions by

Thatcher and Tony Blair – neoliberal individualism was said to now be "in workers' heads".

Yet, against such accumulated pessimism, since the summer of 2022 we have seen a return of strikes, and the beginnings of a rediscovery of the potential power of workers once they move into action.

This potential power has not, so far, been fully realised. Indeed, a central theme of this book is that decisive victories in the major national disputes, so far at least, remain elusive and that the approach of the trade union bureaucracy has been the major constraint that has shaped the confrontations between workers, employers and the government. The question of how to overcome this limitation is the central question that must be addressed if the revival of the working-class movement is to deepen and advance.

What's driving the new strike movement?

What created the impulse for the revival of strikes we have witnessed? The most immediate reason was the end of decades of low inflation. In 2022 inflation hit a 40-year high with the Retail Price Index measure of inflation at over 12 percent by the summer of 2022 – a year previously, it stood at under 4 percent.

But the hike in inflation also took place after an unprecedented period of wage suppression. Wages have been under a sustained squeeze since the financial crisis of 2008, and they have still not recovered to the level they were at a decade and a half ago. A protracted squeeze on pay of this magnitude is without precedent. This is why many of the recent strikes, in the health service for example, bring up the need to not just stay ahead of rising inflation but to seek restoration for falling levels of pay over the past decade. Rising inflation is the straw that broke the camel's back and provoked a fightback.

Alongside rising prices were rising profits – and huge handouts to wealthy shareholders. The Unite union estimated that 350 of the biggest firms saw their profit margins rise sharply during the pandemic, standing at 73 percent higher in 2021 than 2019.

This made workers feel more embittered about eroding living standards and also less immediately fearful for their own jobs, hence more confident to fight back. It also had an ideological impact as the old argument that workers' wage demands push up prices fell flat. When Boris Johnson tried to invoke the spectre of a "wage-price spiral" to oppose the rail and other strikes in the summer of 2022, such claims stood at odds with workers' experiences and lacked even superficial credibility.

The cost of living crisis created a sense of a common experience across the working class, a mood of generalisation that evoked broad sympathy with those groups of workers fighting back, and a sense that they are fighting for all workers.

The outbreak of strikes was also shaped by the pandemic. A common thread connecting many of those who initiated the summer strikes was recognition that, through the height of the pandemic, when millions of workers began working from home and others were placed on the furlough scheme, they were told to work as normal. The government described them as doing "essential work": collecting refuse, delivering to supermarkets, running the transport system, delivering the post, working in the ports and working in the NHS – often a harrowing experience. These essential workers continued their work routines despite the all too real risks from Covid-19 to their health and their lives.

Being called on to make sacrifices for the common good, and often accepting pay freezes during the first phase of the pandemic in the "national interest", led to a tide of anger when the lockdowns ended and profitable firms offered below-inflation pay deals. However, the experience of the pandemic also served to boost such workers' sense of their own power. After all, being told your work is so vital to the continued basic functioning of society that you must work during a lockdown undermines the notion that you are "disposable".

This feeling was, in turn, amplified when the drive rapidly to reopen the economy in autumn 2021 exposed major labour shortages, for example, skilled heavy goods vehicle drivers. Tight labour markets in areas of the economy further boosted some groups of workers' confidence that they could fight and win their demands.

More overtly political factors also played a part in driving the new strike movement. The period in which Jeremy Corbyn was leader of the Labour Party was contradictory. It created a bigger and more confident left, but it also offered a focus away from workplace organisation or even street protests. The focus on getting Corbyn's Labour elected to government, and the internal battle with Labour's right wing, came to dominate everything.

Corbyn's defeat and Labour's shift to the right under his successor, Keir Starmer, has weakened the hold of such electoralism, at least temporarily. Meanwhile, Starmer's desire to prove to the wealthy and powerful that Labour is a safe pair of hands that can be trusted not to threaten their interests has seen him sharply distance Labour from the strikes. So the Labour leadership has refused to endorse pay rises that match inflation and Starmer told his front bench spokespeople not to attend picket lines.

The argument that the priority must be campaigning for – and waiting for – a Labour government to solve the cost of living crisis gained less purchase among union activists and even some sections of union leaderships and officials. For many of those who once looked to Corbyn, the picket line, rather than the parliamentary arena, suddenly seemed to offer a far better solution to the assault on living standards.

The union bureaucracy and "stop-start" strikes

If the first phase of the strikes was marked by the sheer scale of the enthusiasm and picketing, then the second phase was the way the strikes developed into an entrenched episodic, stop-start pattern that limited the pressure they placed on employers and the government.

This reflected the fact that the pace of the disputes was set from above by the trade union bureaucracy. The union leaderships called a typical pattern of one-day strikes, occasionally a few more but often with large gaps between rounds of action.

So the RMT's opening salvo across the rail network involved three days in quick succession in June (21, 23 and 25), but the next strike was not for another month and was limited to one day on 27 July. Two one-day strikes were then called in mid-August, and two more days planned for mid-September, but the latter were rapidly called off when the Queen's death was announced on 8 September.

In the dispute at BT Openreach, the CWU (Communication Workers Union) called a first round of action on 29 July and 1 August, and then a 48-hour strike a month later. But then there was no further action until 6 October.

In Royal Mail, the CWU struck on 26 and 31 August, then held a 48-hour strike on 8-9 September, but the second day was cancelled after the Queen's death. The next strike was not until 13 October.

Aslef also struck on a similar tempo, but limited to a day at a time, with strikes on 30 July, 13 August and 1 October. A strike that had been announced for 15 September was cancelled.

The strikes were powerful and well supported. But their episodic nature meant that employers and the government could seek to ride them out in the hope that the strikers' enthusiasm would wane as financial hardship mounted and the public would lose patience with the disruption that the strikes involved.

Increasingly, even this intermittent tempo was disrupted as strikes were cancelled or postponed for a succession of reasons – the Queen's death was far from the only example. As unions launched re-ballots to allow their strike mandate to extend another six months, strikes were often wholly unnecessarily put on hold. The RMT rescheduled a strike due to a clash with the Royal British Legion's poppy day appeal. But most typically, strikes were called off, or no further action called, simply to take up an offer of talks with employers, even without offers on the table.

When such caution delivered little, some union leaderships were willing initially to step up the tempo a notch. Around Christmas, both the RMT and CWU in Royal Mail did call more sustained action. The RMT called four 48-hour strikes over Christmas and the New Year (after taking no action for nearly ten weeks) and a further three days at Network Rail to hit the key maintenance period starting from Christmas Eve. In Royal Mail, the CWU called six days in total in the critical two weeks in the run-up to Christmas. Yet despite the huge impact and increased pressure these strikes led to, the brakes went back on immediately afterwards with no further action called as both union leaderships looked for talks, once again relieving pressure on employers.

And as more unions joined the strike movement, this patten of episodic strikes prevailed. The RCN, for example, struck on 15 and 20 December but pulled out different NHS trusts on each day, the EIS struck in Scottish schools on 24 November, then at all primary schools on 10 January and all secondary schools the following day. The PCS, despite getting 100,000 members over thresholds in early November, focused on calling out particular groups (driving examiners, border force and the passport office, for example) and only called its first national action on 1 February. The NEU took action on 1 February, with regional strikes in late February and early March then a 48-hour strike in mid-March.

Yet without any actual concessions from employers that could be presented as positive gains, the union bureaucracy had little room to manoeuvre. However much opportunities to "get round the table" were seized on and strikes paused for "intensive negotiations", without any concessions resulting from these talks, the pressure remained to return to calling at least some strikes.

Deals and retreats

The government's initial stance was one of facing the strikes down and refusing to offer any concessions while seeking to turn public opinion, via the mass media, against the strikes as "greedy" and disruptive. Yet by Christmas, and as health workers began to take to the picket line, a deeply unpopular Tory government recognised that it had failed to win the argument throughout society over the strikes, and it shifted tack. It now sought to engage the trade union bureaucracy in deals with very limited concessions, invariably far short of the strikes' original demands, to try and settle the disputes. Thus, the third phase of the strikes was one of limited deals and retreats from further action.

So, initially the government insisted that pay awards for 2022-3, typically at around 5 percent (though just 2 percent for its own direct employees in the civil service), made by the supposedly "independent pay review bodies" could not be revisited. This was while inflation was running at double figures month after month.

But a few weeks into the New Year, the government suddenly discovered it could re-visit these awards. The new offer to NHS staff was a 2 percent one-off payment for 2022-3 on top of the 4 percent already awarded, plus a second additional, but still only one-off, 4 percent "Covid recovery bonus". The award for 2023-4 would be 5 percent, amid much government assertion that inflation would fall sharply by the end of the year. It was also highly unclear whether the money for these offers would come from new NHS funding or come out of existing budgets, leading to yet further service cuts. This was enough for Unison, the RCN and the GMB to recommend these offers in a ballot of members.

This strategy, offering additional one-off payments for one year alone, together with trying to lock unions into two-year deals well below the current rate of inflation, and without providing adequate funding, set the pattern for government offers elsewhere.

So, for example, in April, following four days of action the NEU had called in the spring term, the government offered teachers in English schools an additional one-off payment of £1,000 for the current school year and 4.5 percent for the majority of teachers in 2023-4, with only 0.5 percent of this funded with new money. Some employers had already moved to this strategy of offering modest concessions on strike deals with the union leaderships, which would then present them to the membership as the best they could get.

In BT, after nine days of action in 2022, CWU leaders recommended an offer of a £1,500 flat rate increase, despite the fact that it was the imposition of this same amount earlier in the year that provoked the unprecedented strike vote in the first place. But without a plan for escalation many members couldn't see any alternative but to accept, however reluctantly. Nevertheless, nearly 20 percent voted to reject the offer.

In March, the RMT leadership recommended an offer at Network Rail of 5 percent for January to September 2022, plus an additional 4 percent for the following 15-month period. Coupled with this was acceptance of increased "flexibility" under the banner of "Modernising Maintenance", meaning more night and weekend working and the loss of 1,950 frontline posts. A commitment to no compulsory (as opposed to voluntary) redundancies was agreed, but only till 2025.

Again, after a long drawn-out dispute with little sign of any escalation, and without an organised campaign by militants to reject the offer, many members saw no alternative but to accept. However, like BT, a sizeable minority still held out, with 24 percent voting to reject.

After the strikes that led up to Christmas Eve, the CWU leadership was increasingly desperate for a deal. But, whereas in the past Royal Mail managers had often been willing to retreat and compromise, sometimes simply faced with strike threats backed by huge CWU ballot votes, this time Royal Mail management was determined to impose a serious defeat on the union and, crucially, to weaken the power of the union's workplace reps, the backbone of its organisation. As well as seeking to remove CWU reps' key power to veto "revisions" to local delivery routes, Royal Mail launched a wave of attacks on reps, leaving hundreds suspended or sacked.

The CWU leadership seemed increasingly paralysed as no deal was emerging. Yet it was unwilling to turn back to strikes – and in mid-April, after no strike action for four months, the CWU announced a terrible deal with Royal Mail. This combined what *Socialist Worker* rightly described as a "'surrender'" over pay, with just a 10 percent increase over three years, alongside a raft of attacks on jobs and conditions. The fate of the victimised reps was left to a review to be chaired by Lord Falconer, a former lieutenant of Tony Blair.

Thus, the picture overall was one where a limited strike strategy pursued by the union leaderships in some cases, not all, did extract concessions over pay but invariably below inflation, sometimes significantly so. Moreover, this was the picture regardless of whether the union leadership was seen as "moderate", such as Unison, the RCN or GMB, or seen as on the left, such as the RMT and CWU.

Contesting the bureaucracy

Was there an alternative to this pattern of limited strikes winning, at best, limited deals that failed to match inflation? The Socialist Workers Party (SWP) and others put forward a number of arguments about two forms of escalation.

Co-ordination of the strikes

There has been a big gap between the rhetoric from union leaders about co-ordinating strike dates and the reality on the ground. So, despite resounding talk of co-ordination at TUC Congress in September – and despite the popularity of the idea of "striking together" among strikers on the picket lines – the actual experience of co-ordination has been limited and partial.

On 1 October, all three rail unions plus the CWU in Royal Mail (but not in BT), around 170,000 workers, struck together and this coincided with strikes at both Felixstowe and Liverpool docks.

The CWU leadership had set up a campaign, Enough is Enough, to raise political support for the strikes – not least due to the utter disinterest from the Labour leadership. This saw a huge response with up to 500,000 (and maybe even a million) signing up to it and a number of massive launch rallies in London, Manchester, Leeds, Liverpool and elsewhere. On 1 October, the campaign called a series of local protests in a number of towns and cities (unfortunately, this promising initiative was then put on ice by the CWU leadership and has been largely invisible since).

But it took four more months, until 1 February, for the next major day of co-ordinated action, when the NEU, UCU in the universities and the first national action by PCS coincided. This opened the door to local union branches to come together and call rallies, something the

NEU in particular pushed for. These were sizeable and often electrifying, with reports of 40,000 marching in London, 6,000 in Sheffield, 5,000 in Liverpool, Manchester and Bristol, 2,000 in Nottingham and hundreds in a swathe of smaller towns.

In total, around half a million workers took action on the same day. But it could have been bigger still. The rail unions and the CWU in the post, at the time locked into talks, stood aside and didn't call action. But perhaps most significant was that the health unions did not join in, with the RCN preferring to strike a week later. This reflected a sectional logic that saw some bureaucracies decide that their interests lay with pursuing talks at the expense of action, or striking separately to pitch for "special status" for their particular demands. Something similar happened again on 15 March, when the NEU, PCS and junior doctors in the BMA (British Medical Association) struck together – but the CWU, RMT and other health unions did not.

The co-ordinated action that did take place – particularly joint demonstrations by strikers – did provide a boost to the confidence of those in dispute, strengthening the feeling they were part of a wider revolt, and not locked in isolated disputes. And though co-ordinated action still remains in the hands of the trade union leaders, when it happens it opens up more space for local activists to come together to discuss joining rallies, marches and, potentially, the next steps.

Hard-hitting action

If there was at least a willingness by some trade union leaderships to co-ordinate strikes, arguments for calling longer or more frequent strikes – potentially indefinite strikes – to increase significantly the pressure on employers, were firmly rejected by those same leaderships.

Yet, as Joseph Choonara noted in the pages of *International Socialism*, where much more hard-hitting strikes took place in a number of the more local disputes, the resulting gains for workers were significant:

> In Liverpool, 580 striking dock workers in the Unite union won pay rises ranging from 14.3 to 18.5 percent in November, as well as seeing off the threat of compulsory redundancies. This came after workers rejected a 7 percent pay offer and took five weeks' strike action in three blocks.

In the same month, 250 bus drivers at Stagecoach in Hull, also in Unite, won pay rises of about 20 percent after four weeks of continuous action.

At Arriva North West, bus drivers in the Unite and GMB unions announced indefinite action, which lasted for four weeks, rejecting an offer of 9.6 percent. Again, the basis was laid for an inflation-busting pay award, but this time Unite officials suspended the action, without consulting members. With strikes halted, workers ultimately accepted an 11.1 percent deal.

The one national dispute that escalated to indefinite action, when criminal barristers took this step in early September, led to an offer to increase their fees by 15 percent. In fact, for many, especially lower paid junior barristers, even this was not enough and 43 percent voted to reject the deal and fight for more.

The argument put in the big national disputes, though, was that too many members would not support such escalation. With tens or even hundreds of thousands taking part, there was no strike pay available, unlike in the local disputes. It was argued that more than one or two strike days in a monthly pay period would see significant numbers of members opt out of taking action, fracturing and dividing the strikes.

Yet the alternative was the "long haul" approach of the CWU and RMT, where the number of strike days accumulated over months, but never with enough concentrated impact to lead to a breakthrough. A real victory was much more likely if the railways, BT, Royal Mail, the civil service, schools, universities and the non-emergency health services were shut down for sustained periods, or even through open-ended indefinite strikes with no pre-announced end dates, as this would have precipitated major crises for employers and the government. The pressure to make major concessions would have been far greater.

If union leaderships had put this case in a serious way, reps and activists in every workplace would have had the confidence to carry these arguments into the membership. This would have needed to be combined with efforts to build big picket lines that actively sought to approach anyone thinking of breaking the strike to try and persuade them to reconsider, seeking to win over as many as possible to adhering to the strike.

A strategy offering a credible path to victory can win support despite potentially greater upfront financial sacrifice. Strikes that start to feel like they are going nowhere, on the other hand, can rapidly breed passivity and disillusionment, as the expectation of getting a result that would outweigh the financial losses from the strike fades.

With many strikers taking action for the first time, or with only very limited previous experience of major strikes, the arguments for escalation were listened to respectfully where they were put by socialists. But most strikers hoped employers and the government would back down without taking such steps. Over time, discussions about alternatives to the "long haul" approach, the slow drawn-out strikes with occasional action that is preferred by union leaders, could gain a bigger hearing.

In one union, the UCU, arguments for substantial escalation both had a much wider audience and developed an organisational expression. UCU activists in Higher Education have taken dozens of strike days in several rounds of action since 2018 (including a revolt against the then leader Sally Hunt over a poor deal in the 2018 USS pensions dispute).

After an initial three days of strikes in November 2022, activists associated with the UCU Left and the wider UCU Solidarity Movement successfully won a vote for a move to indefinite action at the union's Higher Education Committee. This, however, was pushed back to 18 days over two months after the general secretary, Jo Grady, and officials manoeuvred to pressure a retreat from the decision for indefinite action. In mid-February, Grady went on to "pause" even this action for talks and subsequently a vote on an offer. Activists have had repeatedly to clash with Grady's attempts to demobilise and put poor offers out to the vote.

The experience of several waves of strike action over the past five years has created a sizeable body of militants in the UCU able to at least contest the direction of disputes and, crucially, at times stop disastrous retreats. But events in the RCN show that networks of opposition to the bureaucracy can develop more rapidly than this.

The RCN leadership mobilised for a ballot and strikes to push their demand for a 19 percent pay claim, to address not just current inflation but to begin restoration of the value of nurses' pay that has been hit by derisory pay settlements over the past decade. Their decision to recommend the government's offer, way below inflation, was met with widespread anger. But significantly a network of activists both around the SWP and around the Facebook page "NHS Workers Say No", which had emerged in opposition to the government's failures in the health service during the pandemic, held online meetings and campaigned against accepting the deal. The resulting 55 percent majority to reject the offer shocked the government and pushed the RCN to call more strike dates.

A central lesson from these experiences is that resisting poor deals is connected to the argument for escalation, which is a break from the limited pressure of episodic strikes. The question of how more can be won, how real victories can be best achieved needs to be raised constantly. This in turn needs to be combined with rebuilding activist networks that understand they cannot rely on the trade union leaderships to fight effectively and consistently.

Alongside this and connected to it is rebuilding traditions of mass participation and collective decision-making in disputes. Mass picketing is not just about putting more pressure on those thinking of breaking a strike. It ensures strikers are not left passive, and isolated at home, that they are part of a collective experience and can see the level of support for a strike. Mass participation in picketing also provides the basis for collective discussion, both informally on picket lines but also in mass meetings or afterwards in a bar or café. These can be places to organise and plan further action, but also to debate next steps, and discuss what kind of action needs to be taken.

One important development in the strike movement was the call by the NEU for strike committees to be established in every area. Such bodies can help easily and rapidly to draw in new activists inspired by the experience of the strikes and help to strengthen the organisation of strikes on the ground in a locality – clearly something the NEU leadership grasped. But strike committees also have the potential to develop into places where the direction of a strike is debated and contested, if necessary clashing with the union leadership. Already, some UCU branches and activists have developed strike committees precisely in order to do this.

For more than 30 years, the near universal experience of working-class activists, even the most militant, has been one of relying on and operating within a framework set from above – by the trade union bureaucracy, and acting independently of them has been a rare exception. So it is not surprising that many activists entered the recent strikes with illusions both about the scale of the confrontation needed to achieve decisive victories over employers and government but also, and correspondingly, the scale of the challenge with their own officials that this would require. But it is from the experiences of strikes themselves that networks of militants who grasp this clearly can start to be rebuilt. The aim of revolutionary socialists must be to help foster and accelerate this process.

Chapter 2: What is the trade union bureaucracy?

The central division in society is between those who own and control the means of production – the capitalists – and those who don't. This second group is made up overwhelmingly of the working class, with some middle-class elements. This divide plays out in every workplace in the battle between the bosses and the workers and their organisations. It is the root of class struggle, strikes, and the growth of trade unions as defensive organisations.

Socialists are on the side of those who fight those at the top of society, the owners and their bloated henchmen. We back strikes and unions, and seek to make those struggles as effective as possible. But, as the earlier chapter showed, there has been a central problem in the strikes of 2022-3 – the failures by trade union leaders.

Following close to 40 years of defeats, the trade union movement – and perhaps especially the leaders of the unions in Britain – entered this new period with a deep pessimism about workers' ability to win substantial victories. At the level of union officialdom, with this pessimism came also a disbelief in the willingness of workers to fight militant struggles.

Trade union leaders were, and are, sceptical about workers' capacity to engage in anything more than token struggles unless sustained by full strike pay that compensates for lost wages. They cower in the face of anti-union laws, frequently refusing to contest alleged breaches of law in court, let alone hold "illegal" walkouts and mass pickets. They know their power is based on workers' organisation, and at conferences and boozy socials talk about the wonders of the workers' fight. But in their hearts many think the employers and the state have the whip hand.

Workers and activists involved in industrial strike action and trade unionism can often find trade union leaders' actions that hold back struggle discouraging and disorientating. These people, after all, are supposed to be on the side of the workers, not their bosses. They are elected representatives of the union, so why do they limit or call off strike action? And it's not just one section of trade union leaders who act like this. Pat Cullen, a so-called right-wing trade union leader of the RCN, and Jo Grady of the UCU, a leader who emerged out of organised left-wing opposition to the previous general secretary, operated in virtually indistinguishable ways in the strikes of 2022-3.

A separate social layer

By the trade union bureaucracy, we mean the full-time officials who derive their living from their union job. They have a different social position to ordinary rank-and-file union members. Socialist Workers Party founder member Tony Cliff wrote:

> The bureaucracy balances between the two main classes in society – the employers and the workers. Top trade union officials are neither employers nor workers. Union offices may employ large numbers of people, but it is not this that gives the union official his or her economic status. On the other hand, the union official does not suffer like the mass of workers from low wages, being pushed around by the employers, job insecurity. The trade union bureaucracy is a distinct, basically conservative, social formation.

This theory says trade union leaders and the full-time employees of the unions constitute a separate social layer with its own set of interests distinct from workers on the one hand and the bosses who oversee and enforce their exploitation on the other. They become negotiators, balancing between workers and bosses rather than class fighters looking to end exploitation altogether. They seek compromise and cannot be relied on to lead struggles. They pull back from militant strikes and have repeatedly led these strikes to defeat or accepted deals far short of what could be achieved.

Cliff said about the bureaucracy:

> Like the God Janus it presents two faces: it balances between the employers and the workers. It holds back and controls workers' struggle, but it has a vital interest not to push the collaboration with employers and state to a point where it makes the unions completely impotent. For the official is not an independent arbitrator. If the union fails entirely to articulate members' grievances, this will lead eventually either to effective internal challenges to the leadership, or to membership apathy and organisational disintegration, with members moving to a rival union.

Trade unions emerged under capitalism as organisations formed by the collective action of workers to resist their own exploitation. They are, however, deeply contradictory social forms, shaped by the frameworks and limits of the capitalist system. They exist to resist the exploitation of workers under capitalism, but they rely for their continued existence on the capitalist system of wage labour.

They do not aim to end the exploitation inherent within capitalism but to improve the terms of this exploitation through a struggle over higher wages and better conditions. So, they give expression to workers' resentment but also contain workers' struggle. Trade union officials become a conservative bureaucratic layer pulled between the demands of the mass of members and those of the bosses.

This is why union leaders and officials are some of the most forceful voices arguing that strikes and trade union campaigns have to be kept inside the confines of legality; even if that legality is completely limiting to the aims of the dispute. Various waves of anti-union laws that have been brought in have shrewdly targeted union funds as punishment if these laws are broken. The threat of fines or asset freezes are the most serious threat of all to union leaders. This often holds them back from pushing for action that can threaten opponents, such as occupying a workplace or secondary picketing.

Material benefits

The union officials' social role is crucial. But there are also clear material reasons for becoming compromisers. They do not experience directly the same exploitation as the workers they represent and in fact draw their usually healthy salaries from the union itself. In July 2022, the government's official trade union monitor issued a list of the pay and benefits enjoyed by trade union general secretaries during the previous year. It makes interesting reading:

Union	Pay (£)	Benefits (£)	Total (£)
Aslef	106,226	27,887	134,113
CWU	104,315	26,051	130,366
GMB	222,000	37,000	259,000
NEU	109,500	23,400	132,900
RMT	109,542	39,802	149,344
RCN	175,538	14,189	189,727
Unison	119,513	12,756	132,269
UCU	104,841	22,121	126,962

Source: Certification Officer for Trade Unions and Employers' Associations, Annual Report 2021-22

The selection above doesn't include the real whopper of the Professional Footballers' Association (PFA) whose general secretary collected a thumping £3,098,382 in pay. In almost every case the present general secretary might say their package is slightly different. Mick Lynch of the RMT has repeatedly insisted he is now paid "only" £84,000 a year, plus national insurance, tax and pension contributions. Sometimes there are special features – the RCN figures, for example, include a payment made in respect of the general secretary's role as chief executive of the RCN Charter Body as well as trade union duties. But it's also true that in many cases these six-figure sums will have soared further as general secretaries make sure they try to keep up with inflation.

These salaries and perks are not in the same league of the titans of industry, or even the very top politicians. But nor are they anything like the sums that ordinary workers collect. The general secretary can enjoy a nice house (possibly two), plush holidays, swanky travel and a secure future based on the union shelling out big pension contributions. They won't ever get to the supermarket checkout and worry whether they can afford the bill. And there's a world of dinners, and top-notch travel on expenses, clothing allowances and invites to plush events that ease the pressure on their bank accounts.

And once they leave the post, in the future, lucrative consultancies, positions on global bodies and government commissions await. And if they aren't on offer, there's always the House of Lords – as Baroness O'Grady of Upper Holloway (former Trades Union Congress general secretary), Baron Woodley of Wallasey (former joint general secretary of Unite), Baron Morris of Handsworth (former leader of the Transport and General Workers' Union) and many others can testify.

General secretaries exist in a different financial world to their members – although the leader of the PFA can claim to be a pauper compared to some of the professional footballers he represents, despite the fact most receive well below his income. The top bureaucrats are suspended between a worker's wage and a chief executive's haul. Some stop their pay when their members strike. Others don't. But urging members to accept a deal far below inflation doesn't affect their own pay.

If you are in a union, do you know how much your general secretary is paid? It's well worth discovering the latest figures and all the benefits that are declared. Just as it would be good if the media were to flash on screen the pay of the business figures, bankers and politicians they interview who tell workers to tighten their belts, it would be positive to have the general secretary's loot revealed when they recommend a deal involving real-term cuts for their members.

Negotiating the terms of exploitation

As unions grow, they set up bureaucracies whose job is to negotiate compromises with employers. Early Labour Party members Sidney and Beatrice Webb described how this process first happened in Britain during the late 19th century. They talked of "a shifting of leadership in the trade union world from the casual enthusiast and irresponsible agitator to a class of permanent salaried officers expressly chosen from out of the rank-and-file unionists for their superior business capacity".

They argued that this led to a situation where "the actual government of the trade union world rests exclusively in the hands of a class apart, the salaried officers". The bureaucrats' instinct is always to seek a settlement where "both sides come halfway". In some disputes such a bureaucratic approach can get results. If the bosses have a bit of slack and don't see the dispute as very significant, concessions can be won without major battles.

It was possible during the long capitalist expansion of the 1950s and 1960s to have both growing profits and growing wages. The strength of the trade union movement in this period combined with high profit rates meant that, if workers pushed, bosses were more than willing to grant concessions. Both Tory and Labour governments granted reforms that improved working-class living standards.

But when the system's crisis squeezes profits, as happened in the period following the Great Financial Crisis of 2007-8, there is much less room for manoeuvre. Bosses attack wages and jobs and expect workers to foot the bill for the crisis. In Britain, the austerity programme launched by George Osborne in 2010 slashed public sector pay in real terms while intensifying both New Labour and Tory neoliberal drives to privatisation.

In times like this, trade union officials can often accept or even echo government or bosses' lines about the unaffordability of workers' demands for higher wages. Dave Ward of the CWU has said that he understands that Royal Mail is in "a serious financial position" and Pat Cullen has talked of the "economic climate" that has to be considered – meaning she would be prepared to accept a pay rise for nurses of almost half their original early 2023 demand.

A century ago, the German revolutionary Rosa Luxemburg wrote of how, for the bureaucrat, the trade union organisation "from being a means, has gradually changed into an end in itself – a precious thing, to which the interests of the struggle should be subordinated, from this also comes the openly admitted need for peace that shrinks from great risks and presumed dangers to the stability of the trade unions".

Trade union leaders – left and right-wing – do sometimes encourage a fightback. These officials would have no leverage on the bosses, and no job, without some workers' resistance and organisation. But officials believe militancy has to be kept within strict limits in case it brings the union into direct clashes with the law or the government.

They tell the most militant union members that others are apathetic or reactionary. The official appeals to workers' instincts for "unity" – not to raise solidarity but to limit the struggle.

Tony Cliff summed up the union bureaucracy's position as "both reformist and cowardly". "It dreams of reforms but fears to settle accounts in real earnest with the state (which not only refuses to grant reforms but even withdraws those already granted), and it also fears the rank-and-file struggles which alone can deliver reforms."

The fate of over 800 seafarers summarily sacked by P&O Ferries in March 2022 shows how trade union leaders' insistence on staying within the law can lead to terrible defeat. After P&O sacked its entire workforce of 800 crew members illegally in order to hire cheaper agency labour, the trade union movement expressed an enormous outpouring of anger.

The first instinct of many seafarers was to stay on and occupy the ships. But their union, the RMT, used the threat of losing their redundancy payments to get the workers off the ships. There should have been ship occupations, sit-ins and mass protests that blockaded the ports and stopped the vessels from sailing, with other dock workers walking off in solidarity. Instead, the union pursued a strategy that relied on shaming the company and the Tory government in the press. This put very little pressure on the company or the Tories, leading to bitter defeat. The CEO of P&O openly admitted they broke the law in sacking the workers and faced virtually no consequences.

In countries like Britain, where there is a developed parliamentary system and a bourgeois social democratic party, there is a sharp and decisive separation between workers' economic and political struggles. The trade union becomes the vehicle for driving forward economic struggles, while parliamentary social democratic parties, like the Labour Party, take on the political struggles on behalf of the working class. Both sides of this picture accept a reformist consciousness, that it is possible only to fight and win reforms within the system instead of looking to overturn it.

Most of the union bureaucracy is very closely allied with the Labour Party. The party was born to give a political voice to trade union leaders and (whatever Blair wanted, and Starmer might like) still has strong links with the trade union leaders. Most bureaucrats are individual members of the Labour Party and doggedly defend their union's links with Labour.

This means that when big struggles break out, there is a clash of loyalties. When Labour is out of government, it tells unions that strikes are unpopular and will lose Labour votes. When Labour is in government the pressure is on union leaders to bow to the government, formed by "their" party.

When big strikes happen, the crucial aim for the bureaucracy is to be "in the room", being taken seriously and negotiating. When the CWU bureaucracy unveiled a rotten deal with Royal Mail in April 2023, the union's acting deputy general secretary, Andy Furey, said one of the big gains was: "The CWU is locked into the agreement as we are there – we're going to be involved every step of the way." But what that really meant was union leaders and reps being tied into an agreement that erodes workers' pay and conditions.

If the bosses and government are ignoring the union leaders, or not directly negotiating with them, the union bureaucracy looks to strikes as a way of forcing negotiations to restart. They don't see workers collectively withholding their labour as a strength that demonstrates their unique role within the capitalist system and that can grind that system to a halt. They see it as a means to get bosses back to the negotiating table.

Fear of confronting the system

The role of the bureaucracy is seen most clearly when there are struggles that go beyond battles over wages and conditions and begin to challenge the state. In 1919 the British state was in complete crisis with an enormous level of strikes and class struggle along with mutinies in the armed forces. The British ruling class was facing the gravest threat to its continued rule for a very long time.

Part of the revolutionary wave that shook Europe at the end of the First World War, this was the closest Britain had come to revolution. The leaders of the powerful Triple Alliance of unions (miners, railway workers, dockers, seafarers and other transport workers) were called to speak with prime minister David Lloyd George, who zeroed in on their weak spot – their imprisonment within the system. He said:

> Gentlemen you have fashioned the Triple Alliance of the unions represented by you, a most formidable instrument, I feel bound to tell you that in our opinion we are at your mercy. The Army is disaffected and cannot be relied upon. Trouble has occurred already in a number of camps. We have just emerged from a great war and the people are eager for a reward for their sacrifices, and we are in no position to satisfy them. In these circumstances if you carry out your threat and strike, then you will defeat us. But if you do, have you weighed the consequences? The strike will be in defiance of the government of the country and by its very success will precipitate a constitutional crisis of the first importance, for if a force arises in the state that is stronger than the state itself then it must be ready to take on the functions of the state, or withdraw and accept the authority of the state. Gentlemen have you considered, and if you have, are you ready?

Rather than contemplating a confrontation with the state, the union leaders retreated and worked to dismantle the strikes. Their loyalty to the state and capitalism was absolute and this is the surest sign of their limitations. If asked to choose between maintaining the status quo and leading struggles that could overturn it, they will always choose the road that shores up the system.

In France in May-June 1968, a massive general strike sparked by student revolts rocked the country, eventually pushing president Charles de Gaulle to flee Paris. A path to revolutionary change was possible.

The union leaders in the CGT union federation along with the Communist Party had to work hard to demobilise the general strike and persuade the workers to go back to work in exchange for wage rises and other reforms – reforms that were swiftly taken back once the movement demobilised.

So if even the best left-wing leaders act to slow down, call off or else limit the struggle of workers, the primary strategy for socialists in unions should not be of winning union positions or electing left-wing leaders. We have to build at the base of the unions, at the workplace level where workers experience their exploitation. This is the organisational conclusion of Karl Marx's idea that "the emancipation of the working class is the act of the working class itself".

The next chapter looks at the record of trying to build at a rank-and-file level.

Chapter 3: A brief history of rank-and-file organisation

The conflict between the interests of the rank-and-file and the trade union bureaucracy has led at certain moments in British working-class history to resistance. Workers have created "unofficial" rank-and-file organisations that have challenged the bureaucracy and even been able to act and lead strike action independently of it. Looking to this tradition is essential at any period of renewed militancy.

The Labour Unrest, the First World War and After
It is at the highpoints of workers' struggles that the internal contradictions and tensions between the rank-and-file and the trade union bureaucracy become most obvious. A period of increased industrial struggle between 1910 and 1921 saw the first national rank-and-file movement emerge in key engineering centres of Sheffield and Glasgow during the First World War. This followed a period of huge strikes and battles by miners, dockers and rail workers during the period known as the "Labour Unrest" of 1910-14. The experience of these strikes brought rank-and-file militants into conflict with not only their employers and the state but with the trade union bureaucracy. This imbued a significant layer of rank-and-file militants with important experience of challenging officials, and sometimes of leading struggles independently of them.

A key development took place in 1915, during the First World War, in Glasgow and the surrounding Clydeside region, centred on engineering shop stewards in the giant armament factories in the city. The war saw a huge expansion in arms production and a drive by employers to erode the customs and practices skilled engineers had built up to defend themselves. The government, Labour and the union bureaucracies, including the engineers' own ASE union, struck agreements to oppose strikes and even the right of workers to leave a job without the permission of the employers in the arms sector. This was later given legal force in the Munitions Act of July 1915.

Abandoned by the union officials, in February 1915 Clydeside engineering stewards led an unofficial strike of 10,000 for a pay rise. Faced with opposition from the ASE Executive and even the local District Committee of the ASE, the stewards created a new body to lead this strike, the Clyde Labour Withholding Committee. The historian James Hinton has provided a description of how it operated:

> Every morning mass meetings were held in the areas and the discussions and decisions of the previous day's committee meetings were reported. Every afternoon and evening the committee was in session, taking reports from the areas and considering ways and means of strengthening and extending the strike... The organisation and contacts between the factories and the areas and between the areas and the centre was almost perfect.

The Clyde Labour Withholding Committee faded after the February strike but it was the forerunner of an even more significant body, the Clyde Workers' Committee (CWC), that emerged in the autumn of 1915 and which drew in groups of workers beyond engineering. The CWC emerged out of a fight to release three shipyard shop stewards jailed in October 1915 under the Munitions Act after a strike at Fairfields, a Clydeside shipyard.

Again, James Hinton describes the functioning of the Clyde Workers' Committee:

> From October 1915 until April 1916, when the Committee was smashed by the government, 250-300 delegates met every weekend in a hall in Ingram Street, Glasgow. In addition to the ASE shop stewards who had formed the basis of the Labour Withholding Committee there were delegates from many of the other engineering and shipbuilding trades. There were delegates from the mines, the railways, from the

Co-operative workers, and at least one schoolteacher... The day-to-day work was done by "a small leading committee" elected at the delegate meeting and meeting two nights a week. Two things characterised this leading group. Its members were all shop stewards at one or other of the arms firms which had led the February 1915 strike and were to remain the backbone of the Committee through 1915-16. And they were all socialists.

Hinton comments:

The Clyde Workers' Committee originated in the failure of the union Executives, or District Committees, to place themselves at the head of the militancy of a section of the Clydeside engineers. From the Fairfield's case the more militant of the engineers learned that if the Munitions Act was to be opposed root and branch, it must be opposed by an organisation and leadership able to act independently of the official trade union structures. The February 1915 strike had taught them that this organisation, to be effective, must be a delegate organisation based directly in the factories. Out of this experience the militants formulated and clearly expressed, for the first time, the principle of independent rank-and-file organisation which was to constitute the basis of the shop stewards' movement.

That principle was brilliantly and succinctly expressed by the CWC in a leaflet it issued in November 1915:

We will support the officials just so long as they rightly represent the workers, but we will act independently immediately they misrepresent them. Being composed of delegates from every shop and untrammelled by obsolete rule of law, we claim to represent the true feeling of the workers. We can act immediately according to the merits of the case and the desire of the rank-and-file.

This method of working within the unions but independently of official structures in an organised movement was an extremely important innovation for the British working class. The shop stewards' movement, consisting of assemblies of delegates elected directly from the rank-and-file in the workplace – working alongside those they represent, not isolated from them as union officials are, sharing the same pay and conditions, and subject to recall should they stop representing their members' wishes – was a powerful development, and remains a model for today.

After the government had counter-attacked and broke up the CWC, arresting the leaders and dispersing them around the country an equally effective and powerful Sheffield Workers' Committee was established, and by 1917 a national movement had emerged capable of leading an unofficial strike of 200,000 workers across 48 towns and cities. The key figures in these rank-and-file movements were socialists and many were revolutionaries who went on to play a key role in the founding of the Communist Party in 1920.

By 1920, recession and a steep rise in unemployment weakened shop floor organisation and employers went on the offensive, imposing a series of defeats on engineers, miners and other workers. The backbone of the rank-and-file movement was broken.

By 1923-4 an economic revival saw a recovery in the working-class movement. By now the Communist Party (CP) embodied the best sections of the rank-and-file militants combined with an understanding of the need for a revolutionary party built not just through propaganda, but through intervention in the day-to-day struggles of the working class. Tragically, the CP's initial clarity about the limits of the trade union bureaucracy, even its most left-wing expressions, and its stress on the need to be able to act independently of it were lost in the run up to the decisive confrontation of this period, the 1926 General Strike. This was not least due to the disastrous influence of the rising state bureaucracy in Russia headed by Stalin, reversing the gains of the October 1917 revolution and retreating from the aim of world revolution. The nine day General Strike in May 1926 was called by the TUC over the coal owners' lockout of over a million miners as they sought to impose major wage cuts and longer working hours.

The energy and enthusiasm of the CP during the General Strike was coupled with illusions in the prominent role of a new layer of left-wing union leaders. It suggested that Purcell of the furniture workers, Swales of the engineers and Hicks of the building workers, as well as A J Cook of the miners, would ensure the TUC would act as the effective central leadership of workers in a major class confrontation. This left the CP and tens of thousands of rank-and-file militants utterly unprepared for the TUC's betrayal of the miners – including the left trades union leaders. After nine days, with the strike solid, the TUC called it off and abandoned the miners, who remained locked out for seven months until they were starved back to work.

The post-war boom and rank-and-file militancy

It took until the mid-1930s for the trade union movement to recover from the disaster of the General Strike. Once again, as the economy began to show signs of recovery following the 1929-33 Great Depression, there was some revival of militancy, not only in old centres of working-class organisation such as coal and textiles, but also in the new "light" industries such as vehicle manufacturing, electrical engineering and chemicals. Strikes led by low-paid engineering apprentices in 1937, for example, saw 100,000 engineering workers come out in solidarity. This was the beginning of an important revival that would last into the post-war period.

The return of full employment from the 1940s gave groups of workers considerable bargaining power and confidence. In key sectors, such as engineering, shipyards, printing, the docks and the mines, this led to strong shop-floor organisation capable of calling strikes, often successfully driving local wage rates well above nationally agreed levels. A mass of strikes took place, often in very localised and fragmented form, sometimes not even organised across a whole factory but in just one section. The vast majority of strikes in the immediate post-war decades were unofficial, short and successful. Tony Cliff called it "do-it-yourself reformism", where stewards were able to win important immediate material improvements without relying on trade union officials or the Labour Party to do it for them.

The *International Socialism* journal, for example, in 1960 carried this account of the post-war traditions of rank-and-file organisation among dockers:

> Elected by mass meetings often attended by over 90 percent of the men of a particular control or dock, the committees represent the most progressive and advanced form of organisation yet developed by the dockers. All committee members are subject to immediate recall. During a dispute new members will often be added to the committee, having proved themselves useful to the running of the strike. In between strikes, the committee will often dwindle to a hard core of five to seven members. Immediately a new struggle erupts the committee will call a mass meeting, place itself before the men for re-election and

seek an immediate broadening of its base, asking for other men to be elected to it. This ensures a genuine responsiveness to the needs of the ranks and a responsibility towards them no other form of organisation is capable of providing.

In the course of the strikes the committees are charged with holding frequent report back meetings. Decisions on whether or not to continue the strike, on whether to extend it or not or whether to return to work on certain conditions, have to be ratified by mass meetings of the men, convened by the committees. The committee members are unpaid, all are working dockers and each individual is known to the men who have to decide whether to vote for him or not. This latter point is very important and contrasts with union elections where men are called upon to vote for people they may never have heard of and seldom know really well.

What transformed this mass of small-scale and fragmented strikes, limited mainly to certain groups of workers, into a much more generalised and widespread movement was an offensive by the ruling class, under pressure from growing competition in world markets, to weaken the strength of the stewards and workplace organisation.

A drive to shift bargaining over wages and conditions away from plant level to the national level, and so into the hands of national union officials and away from the stewards was combined with legislative attacks on the unions (partly to force the bureaucracy to clamp down on unofficial strikes) and attempts to curb pay rises through "incomes policies". This was undertaken first by Harold Wilson's Labour government in 1968-9 and then under the Tory government of Ted Heath in 1970-74.

This led to a much more widespread strike movement and in 1972 there was a series of key victories, including the first national strike by miners since the defeat of 1926.

This strike was driven by the rank-and-file. Networks of militant miners, led by Arthur Scargill, organised "flying pickets" that spread out across the country to shut down energy production and the supply of coal. At Saltley Gate in Birmingham in February, the key confrontation came when some 30,000 engineers and car workers in East Birmingham walked out in solidarity with the miners with 15,000 of them marching to join a miners' mass picket that overwhelmed the police and successfully closed the last available stockpile of coal. The government was forced into a humiliating defeat.

The same year, the imprisonment of five dockers for defying a court order to stop picketing provoked an unofficial national docks strike, with dockers then sending out their own "flying pickets" which successfully convinced other groups of workers to strike in solidarity. Faced with a spreading wave of unofficial strikes involving hundreds of thousands of workers, the government rapidly released the five jailed dockers less than a week after they were arrested.

The upsurge in rank-and-file militancy also spread to previously passive sections of the working class. There was a revolt by low paid public sector workers over the Labour government's policy of pay restraint in 1969-70. And in the early 1970s, postal workers, teachers, refuse workers and health workers all saw an upsurge in action and workplace organisation.

A second victorious miners' strike in 1974 delivered the final humiliating blow to the Tories. In these favourable conditions, the International Socialists (IS, the forerunners of the SWP) attempted to launch a national rank-and-file movement to link up the rank-and-file organisations into an overall structure. As Alex Callinicos writes, central to the IS's ability to do this was its growing implantation in workplaces:

> Between 1971 and 1974 IS was transformed from being a predominantly student to a predominantly working-class organisation. Crucial in this process was the decision by the IS conference of May 1973 to build factory branches. By the next conference, in September 1974, IS had nearly 4,000 members and some 40 factory branches. At the same time, IS members in various industries and unions had launched rank-and-file papers whose aim was to group around them militants who did not fully share their ideas but who were prepared to work with them around concrete issues such as higher wages... these papers had by 1973 achieved a small, but nonetheless significant circulation.

IS took the first step towards building a national rank-and-file movement by calling a delegate conference to discuss the prospects of such a movement on 30 March 1974. 500 delegates representing 270 trade-union bodies attended, and set up the National Rank-and-file Organising Committee (NRFOC). A second conference in November of the same year attracted delegates from a larger number of bodies, including 49 shop stewards' committees, despite CP attempts at a witch-hunt. A new, albeit small movement had, it seemed, been born.

Retreats, defeats and the ebb of the rank-and-file

This promising initiative soon, however, came up against the reality that by 1975 rank-and-file strength and organisation had started to wane. The Labour government of 1974 had been elected with a promise to redistribute wealth towards workers, but when faced with the first major economic crisis since the Second World War, sought to contain and discipline rank-and-file militancy and shift the burden of the crisis onto workers' shoulders.

The Labour government worked with the trade union bureaucracy to undermine rank-and-file militancy, successfully imposing wage controls with its "Social Contract". The impact of the efforts by employers to transfer bargaining over pay and conditions away from the shop floor and into national agreements now began to weaken some of the power and influence of shop stewards, while the return of mass unemployment sapped workers' confidence to fight back. The upshot of all this was that the balance of power inside the unions shifted towards the bureaucracy. In 1976-8 workers experienced the first fall in wages since the 1920s.

Thatcher came to power in 1979 and was able to capitalise on the work of Labour in containing and undercutting the power of the stewards and rank-and-file militancy. Her government was determined to roll back the working-class victories of the early 1970s. She pursued a strategy of isolating and taking on key groups of workers one by one alongside the piecemeal introduction of anti-union legislation. Thatcher's government was able to inflict a series of disastrous defeats – steel workers in 1980, health workers in 1982, miners in 1984-5, printers in 1985-6 and dockers in 1989. These defeats, in particular that of the miners after a year-long heroic strike, had a devastating effect on trade union confidence and organisation from which the working class has yet to fully recover.

The defeat of the miners in 1984-5 was not inevitable. A dispute that the Tories thought would be won in weeks took a whole year. The incredible determination of the miners evoked a huge wave of sympathy and solidarity among large layers of workers. But again and again at key moments – in the first days of the miners' strike, pulling flying pickets back from arguing with miners in Nottinghamshire to back the strike or the TGWU calling off a dockers' strike in the early summer of 1984, for example – the union bureaucracy in the NUM, the TGWU and elsewhere threw away opportunities to deliver powerful blows to the Tories. Scargill, now the NUM general secretary, no longer had the organised networks of rank-and-file militants around him to overcome the conservative resistance of the bureaucracy and he held back from going over the heads of the union bureaucracies to argue for independent action despite the huge influence he had among trade union militants everywhere.

The missing element in the strike was the confidence of the rank-and-file to organise independently of the union machine. In the 1972 strike, the NUM general secretary, Joe Gormley, was from the right of the union. Despite this, a huge victory was won due to the high levels of rank-and-file organisation and militancy. Yet, in 1984-5, with Scargill, the most outstanding trade union leader in post-war Britain (whatever his weaknesses), at the head of the NUM, the miners lost because such networks and organisation had been allowed to wither.

After Thatcher

For what is now a whole generation of activists in the workplace, experiences of operating independently of the trade union officials have been very limited.

Rank-and-file militants built a union, the Offshore Industry Liaison Committee (OILC), that led strikes in the North Sea oil and gas rigs in the 1990s after the Piper Alpha disaster killed 167 workers in 1988. OILC was eventually absorbed into the RMT. From the mid-1990s to the mid-2000s, there were repeated waves of unofficial strikes in Royal Mail and a network of militants in this period were grouped around the paper *Postworker*. Some of those militants ended up becoming part of the official leadership of the union and increasingly abandoned any rank-and-file orientation. And there remains an important tradition of action driven by rank-and-file networks in the construction industry that continues to this day.

However, these examples have not gone beyond the relatively small groups of workers involved and the general picture since the 1990s has been one of a low level of strikes and the weakening or total absence of rank-and-file organisation.

Rank-and-file organisation will not simply re-emerge overnight. It will depend on the accumulation of experiences in a renewed period of strikes that demonstrate the limitations of the bureaucracy's strategy and goals, and the belief and confidence that something better is possible. But it also depends on the active intervention of socialists to push for steps that, however modest, expand the weight of the rank-and-file in every dispute.

Expanding participation and democratic control over strikes is vital. This means rebuilding traditions of mass picketing and mass meetings that involve real debate and decision making. It means re-establishing a culture of strike committees, not just as transmission belts for the union officials but as places of argument and strategy, and ultimately elected by and accountable to mass meetings. Campaigns against below-inflation offers endorsed by union leaders, alongside initiatives to put arguments for escalation of action to win real victories, and a willingness to challenge the bureaucracy are all crucial stepping stones to re-creating rank-and-file organisation for a new era.

Chapter 4: The resistance that shook France

The first five months of 2023 in France saw one of the most important workers' revolts in Europe for many decades. Its trajectory had some similarities with Britain's strikes but at a much higher level. At no point did the British strikes seem to raise the possibility of revolutionary change. The ones in France did.

On 7 March, according to the CGT union federation, some 3.5 million people joined 270 demonstrations across the country, including 700,000 in Paris. Nearly a quarter of a million marched in Marseille, a city similar in scale to Birmingham. In Toulouse, the size of Liverpool or Edinburgh, 120,000 came out. In Bordeaux, with a population equal to Cardiff, 100,000 took to the streets. And many of those marching had struck to join the protests. Workers stopped work across swathes of the public and private sector.

And this was just one of at least 13 days of national action – the battle continued as this book was being written. Such protests are on a historically unprecedented scale. They are certainly the biggest since the great revolt of 1968, although the strikes and occupations are far more limited. The numbers on the streets exceeded those in 1936 – a revolutionary situation. The fear of protests was so great that French authorities even called off a long-planned visit by Britain's King Charles III, perhaps mindful of the fate of Louis XVI who lost his head in 1793.

It's important to be reminded that the working class can rise up, can repeatedly defy the political set-up, and can refuse to be intimidated by its police and brutal laws. Again and again, people have refused to go back to "normal life" or to "move on".

And strikes have power. On 19 January, for example, nearly all local and regional train services stopped, buses and trains in cities such as Paris were "very disrupted" and high-speed train lines across the country were not running. The main teachers' union said 70 percent of primary school teachers were on strike, with many schools closing for the day.

Walkouts heavily disrupted public service radio and television which were reduced to playing music or showing repeats. Many theatres closed. Pickets blocked some refineries and energy workers' action cut power supplies. Some school students blockaded their schools, despite the violence of cops wielding tear gas.

It was president Emmanuel Macron's assault on pensions – adding two years to the retirement age and increasing the required contribution period to 43 years in order to claim the full rate – that triggered the uprising. This declaration of social war was an important issue in itself.

On picket lines and protests the slogan "Metro-Boulot-Caveau" was common. It said the pension changes meant "Travel to work, slog away – and then the grave". Workers felt a mixture of bitter anger and fear over being forced to work until they drop.

Dominique, a retail supervisor, told France 24 News in January:

> I have worked in retail for 30 years. I've already had surgery on both shoulders to deal with tendonitis caused by all the repetitive movements and heavy loads. I've also had to get prosthetic thumbs on both hands. I've lost my joints from ripping and tearing boxes to put on shelves. So if I end up being told I'll have to delay my retirement. I won't be able to accept it. I've never gone on a protest or gone on strike in my life – but this time we're coming up against something really unpalatable. If you ask too much of people, it just becomes unbearable for them.

The issue became a focus for much wider grievances. In mid-April Xavier, a postal workers' union rep in Hauts-de-Seine, told the *Reporterre* website he had been on strike since 7 March. How is it possible to manage more than a month without pay, his interviewer asked. "What is not manageable is the society in which we live. I prefer to lose one, two or three months of salary rather than sacrificing two years of my life to die at work," he replied.

Agathe, a rail worker, said:

> The strike doesn't cost me much, it enriches me. I met a lot of people, in actions, in demonstrations. We have forged links with employees from other sectors and that is very valuable in leading the fight. When we stop working, we take the time to think about the social and political organisation of the world, the wealth we create, and what society gives back to us, which is to say almost nothing.

People discovered, or rediscovered, ways to fight. Philippe Poutou from the NPA revolutionary organisation expressed this well:

> Everything becomes possible again. Through the mobilisation – the big protests, declared or unofficial, strikes, blockades – what we see is confidence returning. Once again, we feel that we can act collectively, that we can change things collectively. We can dare to say shit to power, dare to confront all that, lighting garbage cans, demonstrating at the time you want, when you want. We've relearned to act together, to trust each other.

Energy workers didn't just join the strikes and demonstrations but went further and decided who would have power supplies. Sébastien Menesplier, general secretary of the CGT's mines and energy sector, said at the end of January that union members had "massively" carried out "Robin Hood actions" – taking from the rich and giving to the poor – in the Paris region, Lille, Nantes, Lyon, Nice, Saint-Nazaire and elsewhere. The CGT said:

> Several hospitals and clinics, municipal skating rinks and swimming pools, public sports centres, libraries, middle schools, high schools, nurseries, collective heating of universities or low rent housing, public lighting of small and medium-sized towns and social housing have received free electricity or gas.

Other workers cut off Amazon sites and the home addresses of ministers.

One sign of the breadth of support for resistance to Macron is the money raised for strikers. According to figures in *Le Monde* newspaper from Leetchi, an online platform, between 10 January and 13 April, the

149 strike funds it hosted collected 1,644,714 euros (£1,448,000). "This is three times more than what was collected during the 2019-2020 pension conflict," added *Le Monde*. And it is just one platform, and just online. There were many more local funds filled by banknotes stuffed into a collecting box or handed in at picket lines.

All of this went to a qualitatively higher level on 16 March when Macron rammed the pension law change through parliament without a vote. He feared that he would not have a majority if he allowed MPs to have a say so he used Article 49.3 of the undemocratic constitution of the Fifth Republic introduced by general Charles de Gaulle in 1958. This means a measure goes through with MPs approving it unless the government is defeated in a no-confidence vote – which it narrowly survived.

Protesting in Bordeaux, Frank Masal, a maths teacher, said the use of 49.3 was "a form of dictatorship". A poll showed 82 percent of French people believed that the use of 49.3 on this issue was wrong. Young people flooded on to the protests in much greater numbers, enraged by a president arrogantly abandoning even the pretence of democracy.

"King of the rich" on his own

Macron was now massively isolated. The left-wing novelist Joseph Andras wrote in *Mediapart*:

> Almost all active employees reject the pension reform. Never, every investigation shows, has the monarch found himself so isolated. Wherever a Macronist leader goes in the country, he is booed. A Norwegian singer asked her audience in April to teach her two or three words of French, and the audience chorused, "Macron resign". The formula now has cultural heritage value (somewhere between the baguette and Edith Piaf).

It was a challenge not just to Macron but to the hegemony of the ruling class, the lie that it rules as the expression of popular opinion. The Nobel Prize-winning author Annie Ernaux wrote in *Le Monde Diplomatique* that the 2023 events had reminded her of the huge wave of strikes in 1995 when, "I remember an exhilarating feeling of uncertainty, the feeling that I was experiencing one of those rare moments when history is made because for once working people were driving the action."

The state's response was to step up repression. This was not some peculiarity of the Macron regime. Across the world governments in crisis are reaching for more authoritarian measures as they face protests. This hardening of the state's face has meant the police act, the public order bill and the illegal migration bill in the space of two years in Britain. In France in 2023 reports of police firing tear gas, truncheoning protesters, shooting flash ball grenades, using water cannons and sweeping up scores of people in mass arrests became almost commonplace. This was a continuation of the foul treatment of the Yellow Vests from 2018-19. The Yellow Vests, or Gilets Jaunes protests, which began as a movement against fuel price increases, became increasingly radicalised to the left and targeted Macron. He unleashed his forces against it, leading to mass arrests, horrific injuries and the death of a bystander.

Then came the environmental protest in Saint-Soline in western France. Around 30,000 protesters had gathered for a weekend of action against a mega-basins project that would drain water resources to benefit a small group of giant agri-businesses. The state mobilised 3,200 police and gendarmes who fired nearly 4,000 blast grenades in less than two hours. That's about one every two seconds.

They left 32-year-old protester Serge D in a coma and "hanging between life and death". On the eve of the protest the interior minister Gérald Darmanin said, "The forces of disorder will not win and the extreme left will not win." For the government, the possibility of a dead demonstrator was a price worth paying to make sure of that.

The authorities sent helicopters, mounted forces, water cannon, and trucks to surround the contested construction site – and gendarmes on motocross quad bikes. For two hours, cops drowned the protest area with tear gas and fired volleys of GM2L grenades, classified as weapons of war.

Sebastian Roché, research director at the National Centre for Scientific Research (CNRS) said, "We are not in a police state but we have entered a hybrid form, which I call a police democracy, with an elected power that governs through the police by 'squeezing' the intermediary bodies: associations, professional organisations, the parliament."

The state attacks reinforced the process of a "trade union issue" – pensions – overflowing into a broader criticism of the system. The horrors of police repression can intimidate people but radicalise others – as happened with large sections of Yellow Vests.

A fundamental assault on the working class, opposed by 70 percent of people, was coming from a government that was in power as a result of a minority vote in the legislative elections and from a president who won the votes of just 21 percent of registered voters in the first round of the presidential election and who was elected because people gritted their teeth and chose him over the fascist candidate Marine Le Pen. And when people protested, which was supposed to be their right, the democratic state met them with utter brutality.

The protests raised issues of oppression as well as exploitation. Women workers, students and feminist activists were prominent on the demonstrations. It was an important development and clearer than in some previous campaigns. The pension attacks hit women particularly hard because they are on average paid less, and therefore often have smaller pensions. They also take longer to hit the required number of years worked because of breaks for childcare. International Women's Day on 8 March came just as the movement accelerated. The mobilisations helped to extend the strikes that had taken place on a big day of union mobilisation the day before.

Anti-racists also intervened in the demonstrations and strikes. The Marche des Solidarités group from the start inserted the demand to oppose the new anti-migrant law put forward by interior minister Darmanin and, fearful of fighting on too many fronts at once, Darmanin at least temporarily withdrew the measure. Marche des Solidarités said:

> The world today embodied by Darmanin hunts, attacks, kills, expels, discriminates, overexploits and divides on the basis of origin, skin colour, nationality, religion. This world that breaks solidarity also destroys the planet, develops all inequalities and attacks all our rights. This world bears war and fascism. We say that if we do not fight back when one of us is discriminated against, humiliated, repressed, exploited, all our struggles are weakened.

In the context of mass revolt, such a message had wide support.

And yet, and yet. In the early hours of 15 April Macron officially proclaimed the new pension regulations, due to come into force in September 2023. A few hours earlier the tame Constitutional Council, stuffed with mainstream figures, announced that the process of passing the law was within the regulations. The council struck out a few late changes, ironically the ones designed to make it more acceptable, but the core parts went through.

Macron had 15 days after the Constitutional Council ruling to promulgate the new law. But to spit in the face of the union leaders, he did it almost before the ink was dry. And his prime minister Élisabeth Borne said the government would now accelerate other reforms.

The role of the union leaders

Macron has relied on the truncheon, the elite constitution and most crucially on the trade union bureaucracy. Earlier chapters in this book have set out why the union leaders act this way. France in 2023 is a very sharp example. The leaders of the French unions speak in a bolder key than their British counterparts. But their overall performance is equally dire.

They have never fought to create the conditions for the all-out and indefinite strikes needed to win. Macron feared an extended general strike. The union leaders did their best to avoid it. Days of action spaced out and narrowly focused on the single issue of the new law rather than widening out to include pay and other questions tended to exhaust some of the most militant sections without involving new forces.

At an early stage, the unity of France's eight union federations helped to mobilise people. Pressure from below forced the CFDT leaders, the largest but also one of the most conservative union bodies, to call for full support for action. This boosted the numbers. But later this sort of unity meant subordinating the movement to what CFDT leader Laurent Berger wanted.

And he acted as a trailblazer for a sell-out. "We are not in the logic of the indefinite strike, it is not a call for a general strike," he said on 11 February when the joint unions backed a statement to "bring France to a halt" on 7 March. He praised the "dignified and respectful mobilisation" of the protests and added, "We have to go up a notch, in numbers. But we will not fall into violence."

After the law passed, Berger was eager to return to the bureaucracy's job. "When you are in a company, even if your boss has done things that you do not accept, at some point, you go back to discussing when you are a staff representative," he explained. "This is how we defend the workers, not otherwise."

The more militant-sounding leaders, such as those in the CGT federation, used Berger as an excuse for their own failures. They didn't break with the right and were therefore as bad as Berger. When Berger called for "mediation" with the government, CGT leader Philippe Martinez went along with him – which led to outrage at the CGT congress as he spoke. No union leader challenged Berger's assertion that "there is no question of contesting the legitimacy of the Constitutional Council". Neither Martinez nor his replacement Sophie Binet has told workers to fight for a general strike or to jettison leaders such as Berger. So they ended up, as the French phrase has it, "serving the soup" for the right.

The problem for the union leaders is that the government has not "played the game" of talks. Macron has refused compromise even when a section of bosses was unsure about the fury his actions had detonated. The pension attacks are part of unfinished business for the French ruling class. In Britain, Thatcher smashed union power through a series of confrontations culminating in the miners' strike of 1984-5. Ronald Reagan ushered in a "new era" of – non-union – workplace relations by destroying the air traffic controllers' strike in 1981.

None of this was inevitable. In both the British and the US case, the failure by union leaders to offer solidarity to those on the frontline was crucial to the defeats. But the victories for the bosses and their politicians were real.

French rulers had not delivered such successes. Journalist Romaric Godin noted in an interview:

> If we study the introduction of neoliberalism in France, we can distinguish two stages in its development. From 1983, in what is known as the "turn to austerity", we have reforms that focus on the financial sphere and privatisation, but do not directly involve the world of work.
>
> From 2010, there was a direct attack on workers, with pension reforms forced through and labour market reforms in 2015, 2016 and 2017. This occurred despite massive demonstrations and blockades in transport.
>
> Let's be clear: there was no fundamental retreat by capitalists in the face of labour in previous decades! But confronted with a social movement, they found different ways of acting to support the profit rate, which for 50 years had been under very strong negative pressure bound up with the structural decline in productivity.

The financial crisis of 2008, and enhanced global competition, reduced the space for deals and created the conditions for confrontation. And that was made easier by political developments. The terrifying rise of the National Front and then the National Rally of father and daughter Le Pen is a mortal threat to the working class.

But for mainstream politicians, it means that if they make it into the final round of the presidential election they face the far right rather than another essentially similar force. They can play being Republican for a few weeks and then go back to ruling in the interest of profit and using racism to divide opposition – which can help to create the conditions for the fascists to win.

The rank-and-file organise

As the bureaucrats reeled, a challenge came from the rank-and-file networks that in some places delivered indefinite strikes in some refineries, sectors of transport, refuse workers, dockers, energy workers and others. In mid-April, these were too limited to pose a full national alternative to the union leaders. But they gave a glimpse of what was needed. They organised not just within industries but across different areas, often on the initiative of left-wing socialists and revolutionaries.

On a big day of action, the port city of Le Havre was practically shut after workers in the CGT union organised major mobilisations from below to block roundabouts and approach roads. They closed the port area and the entire industrial zone, including the Total refinery, the Renault car plant, Chevron (chemicals) and Safran (rocket and aero engines).

Socialist journalist Arthur Nicola of Révolution Permanente reported that the action began at 5am as strikers and other activists gathered at union headquarters in Harfleur and 6am in Le Havre. "Nearly 1,000 strikers gathered before dividing up to block several points," he wrote.

> On the "Total" roundabout, in the middle of the industrial zone, Stéphane Allegre, an employee of Seita which produces the famous Gauloises cigarettes, explained that the blockade "was decided to take things up a level, to force the government to let go".

Martin, one of the organisers of strikers' networks in Le Havre, told *Socialist Worker*:

> A general assembly of strikers across all sectors on 7 March with workers from many sectors and factories allowed us to discuss the mobilisation

and the renewal of the strikes at local level. On Tuesday we had 45,000 at our demonstration. Then on Wednesday we organised from 4.30am to block the refuse truck depot. At 10.30am we left to support a comrade who, because of his organising, had been summoned for a preliminary interview that could go as far as dismissal. At 6pm we had a demonstration for International Women's Day. Then on Thursday, we were out with the students at the university.

Workers at the Enedis electricity distribution network near Bordeaux set up a "struggle headquarters" so "all the workers opposed to this reform can come to converge and exchange, talk about actions beyond the demonstrations and hit the economy".

As early as 7 February, Alexis Antonioli of the CGT Total Normandy said:

> For us there is a radicalism at the base on which we must rely to build the indefinite strike. The union leaders don't want to go there. They have a slow calendar. We have to get out of the framework of 24-hour calls and couple it with actions such as blockades.

The Autonomie de Classe revolutionary socialist group said early in the movement:

> After mobilisations of a scale unprecedented since the 1995 victory against the government and anger that goes far beyond the sole pension reform, a question will be reverberating in all conversations of those who take part in the fight in the streets, the meetings, workplaces and education. How to win?
>
> The ruling class is determined. The world they rule is collapsing, and they will do anything to preserve it. Acceptance or revolt are the two poles between which the majority of our class oscillates and has not yet settled. We need to increase the determination to strengthen the one of the revolt, which means devoting a strategy that paves a path to win.

On 26 March rank-and-file workers' solidarity and militancy headed off an attempt to break the strike at the largest refinery in France. The government had requisitioned some of the strikers at the Normandy refinery, giving Total the power to order them back to work or face fines and jail.

The CGT Total Normandie called all the union members in Le Havre to a rally in front of the refinery at 8pm. Over 300 strikers from all the industrial areas of the region – dockers, ports, rail workers, Chevron and others – as well as students turned out. They stood outside the site all night to stop any return to work and to prevent police assaults on the pickets. When bosses tried to negotiate with the strikers, offering to lift the requisitions if the workers agreed to end the strike, the pickets refused outright.

Such examples undermine the idea that there was no alternative to the union leaders' strategy. But the failure to generalise such struggles may mean that Macron escapes the ejection he so richly deserves. It's already clear that workers have learned valuable political lessons and some employers will be wary about taking on those who have mobilised in such numbers. The ruling class will also be divided over whether to keep pressing on with attacks. As in all working-class struggles, the argument will be either "it was a mistake to rise up" or "next time, let's do it better". Positively, the second of those is likely to be dominant.

But the confinement of the movement by the union leaders restricted the victories that were possible. As they abandoned their all-out strike in mid-April after six weeks, Normandy refinery workers issued a bitter but defiant press release:

> If the mobilisation struggles today, it isn't for lack of determination on the part of the base, which has been on strike for weeks, but because the inter-union [body of trade union leaders] has refused to build a balance of power to match the ambitions of our enemies. Rather than calling for seven days of action since 7 March, they should have called for these days of strikes to be linked together to truly stop the economy, which would have changed the movement's destiny… We are among those who never believed in the method of isolated days of action.

In the presidential election of 2022, left-winger Jean-Luc Mélenchon won over 7.7 million votes. His LFI (La France Insoumise) party was at the centre of the NUPES coalition involving LFI, the Communist Party, the Greens and the Labour-type Socialist Party that achieved 6.5 million votes and won 131 MPs at the parliamentary elections that followed.

However, support for Le Pen's National Rally (RN) has risen during the recent revolt. The union leaders' actions are the crucial background to understanding why. There was a real chance to undermine the fascists. Polls showed that those who voted for Le Pen in 2022 were as likely as those who voted for Mélenchon to say they supported escalation of the strikes. And similar numbers said they understood why people fight the police. For opportunistic reasons Le Pen has always been careful to say she does not back the pension changes but she did not back hardening the strikes, and always lined up with the police. There was a chance to drag sections of her voters away from her.

The key is to widen the struggle and make it win. Instead, sections of the left think the problem is that the movement has gone too far. For example, Socialist Party MP Philippe Brun claims that the noisy protests in parliament by MPs in Mélenchon's LFI drive voters to the RN. "The outrageous side of LFI keeps us away from power," he said. Others argue there is a difference between the "hot anger" of the demonstrators and the "cold anger" of those who don't like Macron but don't strike and march and therefore gravitate towards the far right.

Even if there was such a division, it's not necessarily permanent, and the way to break it down would be to make more people active participants in the revolt, not to be more "respectable". Rising class struggle opens the possibility of undermining racism, but it isn't inevitable. It requires feeding the fires of revolt and consciously arguing against racism and Islamophobia at the same time.

Mélenchon's NUPES coalition has not been central to the revolt, despite successes in the presidential and parliamentary elections of 2022, with the coalition winning 6.5 million votes and 131 MPs.

It was aimless and increasingly divided as the revolt grew. While acknowledging the role of unionised workers, Mélenchon has said the crucial actor is "the people". In particular he sought to lead his own movement away from a focus on workers. He wrote, "The rebellious movement must throw all its weight into the mobilisation outside the walls of the company, among the 'non-salaried' people... also middle-class executives and small bosses and traders."

A revolutionary crisis?

How close has France come to a revolutionary situation? People learn in struggle about the hostility of bosses, police, judges, media and government – and the solidarity of allies. Russian revolutionary Leon Trotsky said that revolutions were not about reaching some point on a proletarian struggle thermometer. They are a moment of "the direct interference of the masses in historical events".

A revolutionary crisis develops because of what the exploited and oppressed do in a situation where tensions have ripened to an extent where what they do matters profoundly. To say there is potential in France doesn't mean that a revolutionary uprising is immediately on the cards in France. It indicates that the sweep of resistance is great enough to set in train a process that points towards revolutionary conclusions. Forcing out Macron, for example, would show it is possible to win change beyond elections and formal political mechanisms.

The key is for revolutionaries to be strong enough to advance demands that bring together economic and political struggle through the method of class organisation. They have to be independent of the trade union leaders and the reformist political parties. The aim is to make workers aware of their own potential power and to lead them away from reliance on false hope in parliamentary manoeuvres.

The best demands are those that liberate workers from the straitjacket of "realism". There need to be intensely practical and immediate fights, and those that reach further: in 1917 in Russia, revolutionaries called for land, peace, bread and all power to the workers' councils. Bringing down Macron would direct attention towards abolishing the fiercely undemocratic constitution of the Fifth Republic which allowed the president to impose the pension assaults by decree. This has to set off a process of discussion throughout the working class on what will replace it.

As well as defeating the attempt to raise the pension age, workers would have to fight to reduce it. Freeing themselves from the bureaucratic narrowness of agitating only about pensions, workers would have to call for pay rises for all, full rights to picket and protest, and the removal of the laws that allow the state and corporations to order some strikers back to work with the threat of fines and jail.

This raises the question of leadership. This doesn't mean that if only we had a revolutionary socialist at the top of the CGT union federation there would have been an insurrection in France. Leadership has to be implanted in substantial sections of the working class. Lenin saw the party as the organisation that differentiates a revolutionary situation from a revolutionary crisis. It is the instrument that doesn't just line up a collection of important issues but welds together the fight on all fronts around the spine of workers' power.

At the same time as fighting over workplace issues, revolutionaries in France say workers have to confront the anti-migrant Darmanin law, and all the measures that oppress and brutalise Muslims and black people. At times of deep crisis, the state and its forces become the strategic target. The state is the intersection of political control and the economic dictatorship of big corporations. To undermine state power there should be demands such as the abolition of the ultra-repressive Brav-M (Motorised Brigades for the Repression of Violent Action) unit and the removal of the cops' armoury of grenades and gas. Crucially all of these demands are realisable only through the systematic growth of rank-and-file organisation both in individual workplaces and by co-ordinating between workplaces.

If all these possibilities were fulfilled it wouldn't bring in socialism overnight. But workers would start to see alternative sources of power and decision-making that could destroy and replace the capitalist state. Everything that diverts and delays that process is fatal. It creates openings for the bureaucrats to squeeze life from the struggle. Lenin wrote:

> It is not every revolutionary situation that gives rise to a revolution. Revolution arises only out of a situation in which objective changes are accompanied by a subjective change, namely, the ability of the revolutionary class to take revolutionary mass action strong enough to break (or dislocate) the old government, which never, not even in a period of crisis, "falls", if it is not toppled over.

Chapter 5: Politics, trade unions and strikes

When bosses, media and government ministers attack a strike as "politically motivated", as they have frequently done during the recent strikes, too often union leaders respond by insisting that strikes are solely about immediate issues of pay, working conditions and so on ("bread and butter issues" as they are sometimes described) and are in no way political.

Yet this leaves the wider political and ideological framing of strikes in the hands of the other side which they use to try to weaken support for strikes and demoralise those taking part.

So, opponents of strikes for higher pay claim that "the country can't afford it", and "the money isn't there". And they desperately try to turn other workers against the strikes through divide and rule, with arguments such as, "What about lower paid workers, aren't you making their lives harder?", usually with spurious claims that those on strike earn huge wages.

A strong response to such arguments is when a clear and confident case is put that what happens at work is political. The distribution of wealth between wages and profits, for example, is a political question about the kind of society we live in, as is the question of whether workers should have control over the pace and conditions of work, and what they produce. In services, such as education or health care, arguments about funding, pay and the way, say, schools, universities, or clinical care is organised and in whose interests are major political questions.

Openly accepting that these issues are political would allow a more effective challenge to the logic of those who attack strikes. None of this is new.

Indeed, even during the 1926 General Strike, one of the most open confrontations between workers and a government in working class history, union leaders sought to deny the strike had any political dimension. Stanley Baldwin, the Tory prime minister at the time, went on the attack, declaring that the General Strike was an assault on "constitutional government" and "a challenge to parliament and... the road to anarchy and ruin".

But the response of the TUC and trade union leaders was to vehemently deny this. Instead they insisted again and again that the strike's "sole aim... is to secure for the miners a decent standard of life. The council is engaged in an industrial dispute. In any settlement the only issue to be decided will be an industrial issue, not political and constitutional."

What this translated into, for example, was TUC instructions for pickets not to disrupt or take charge of the movement of goods, and especially food; the government had taken control of this in order to break the strike. Refusal to challenge its control considerably weakened the impact of the strike.

We may not currently face a state directly intervening in mass strike-breaking enforced by police truncheons as in 1926, though in France we have seen something closer to this. But should strikes here escalate, the British state would hardly shy away from doing this (its role during the 1984-85 Miners' Strike makes this clear). Being openly political in our defence of strikes doesn't weaken our struggles, it strengthens them.

In fact, the real problem isn't a total absence of politics from the trade unions but the separation of economics and politics into two distinct spheres. On the one hand, the unions deal primarily with immediate workplace matters, with economic issues of pay rates, working schedules, pensions and so on. On the other, politics is seen as outside the workplace in the realm of elections, parliament and government. And the vehicle in this arena is the Labour Party.

Labour and the unions

The dominant political tradition in the unions is to look to Labour and hope that a Labour government can improve the situation facing workers and trade unions. Indeed, it is often claimed that it was the unions that established the Labour Party at the turn of the last century. But the reality wasn't so straightforward. The real drive for the unions to break their alliance with the old Liberal Party and switch to setting up a Labour Party came from the *trade union bureaucracy*. It was the interests of the bureaucracy that shaped the creation of Labour, not those of the rank-and-file.

The years immediately before and after the turn of the 20th century saw employers successfully impose a series of major industrial defeats on the union movement, which had grown rapidly during the 1889-91 strike wave known as the "New Unionism".

As is so often the case when employers and the state gain the upper hand, they became more confident in pushing for legal constraints on the unions. The Taff Vale judgement of 1901, where a law court ruled that unions could be sued by employers for any loss of profits during industrial action, was a major threat to the funds that sustained the wages, pensions and offices of the trade union bureaucracy itself.

Setting up a Labour Party and breaking from the Liberals was a step forward. But simultaneously it moved the focus away from the workplace and collective action, where the bureaucracy feared the risks of open class confrontation, and into the electoral arena. The Labour Party and a focus on parliament became an alternative to collective workers' struggles.

Getting Labour elected can thus become an excuse for trade union officials not to organise resistance in the workplace – it is presented as an easier option and the only real solution to hostile employers, especially if workers lack confidence in their own strength. And worse, getting Labour elected is said to be more likely if strikes aren't taking place, as Labour feels the need to appeal to the whole electorate and not just trade unionists if it wants to be "electable". And union leaders, in their desperation to get Labour into office, often accept this argument too.

This shifts politics to the realm of the individual citizen, voting in isolation, where we are all supposedly equal citizens regardless of wealth and which side of class exploitation we sit on. A low-paid rail worker or hospital cleaner has the same one vote that the chief executive of a train operating company or outsourced corporation running ancillary services, or even a billionaire, has.

Elections are not where workers' real strength lies. Rather it lies in the collective class-based forms of organisation such as strikes that can disrupt and paralyse the production of goods and delivery of services, halting the flow of profits those chief executives and super-rich utterly depend on.

Starmer: a break from the past?

As noted earlier in this book, one of the factors behind the current strikes has been that the attraction of Labour as a solution to workers' grievances has weakened, at least for now, under Keir Starmer's leadership. After becoming leader in the wake of Jeremy Corbyn's defeat at the December 2019 general election, Starmer's whole strategy has been to move Labour to the right and to reassure the ruling class that a Labour government would be no threat to their wealth and power. He has also sought to try and demonstrate that never again would the left in Labour re-emerge to take the helm of the party.

This has taken the form of a war, not against the Tories, but to crush the Labour left. The removal of the Parliamentary Labour Party whip from Corbyn himself, and subsequently the decision to stop him re-standing as a Labour candidate in the next general election, is simply the most visible expression of this strategy.

But a second strand of Starmer's drive to remove the spectre of Corbynism has been his determination not to identify Labour in any way with the strikes, despite their popularity. Notoriously, Starmer told his front bench spokespeople not to attend picket lines. And the Labour leadership has also avoided calling for pay rises that match inflation. In effect, Labour's official position is to support real term pay cuts. The one Labour shadow minister who committed both these sins – attending a picket line and publicly expressing support for pay rises above inflation – Sam Tarry was summarily sacked as shadow transport secretary.

But even now parts of the union bureaucracy are convinced that getting Starmer into Downing Street is the only way forward. As a general election looms closer, and especially if there are setbacks or worse in the strikes, the pull of electoralism can grow and in turn be used to discipline union activists to hold back militancy and avoid "rocking the boat", which supposedly risks Labour's chances at the ballot box.

Though Starmer's hostility to strikes is in sharp contrast to Corbyn's approach, it is not some radical departure from the Labour Party's past traditions. If anything, it was Corbyn who was the exception to Labour's past record (and even here there are limits that should be recognised).

Of course, many Labour Party members now and in the past have taken part in strikes, supported them and built solidarity for them. But the record of the Labour leadership and especially Labour governments is markedly different.

So, Ed Miliband, seen as to the left of Tony Blair, when asked by an interviewer about his attitude to the 2011 public sector pensions strikes endlessly, like a stuck record repeated the phrase "these strikes are wrong".

During the 1984-5 Miners' Strike, then Labour leader Neil Kinnock (who, like Miliband, came from the soft left of the party) repeated right-wing demands that the miners hold a ballot (not then a legal requirement) to weaken the strike. Kinnock also constantly denounced "violence on both sides" even though it was the police who were systematically attacking miners and their supporters on picket lines, on demonstrations and in mining communities.

Neither Blair nor Miliband nor Kinnock betrayed Labour's traditions. Such responses are precisely the tradition of the Labour leadership. Take another example from what many would consider the "Old Labour" era. In 1966 the Labour prime minister, Harold Wilson, denounced a strike by low paid seafarers as a "strike against the state" led by a "tightly knit group of politically motivated men" – a clear attempt at red-baiting Communists and the left in the midst of the Cold War. Labour introduced a State of Emergency that gave it powers to clear the ports using troops.

In 1969 Wilson's government tried to introduce laws to weaken trade union power known as In Place of Strife (which included the first attempt to impose ballots before strikes could be called). Half a million workers, mostly organised through unofficial networks of activists, went on strike against Labour's plans and sank them.

Or take John Prescott, a former seafarer shop steward and trade unionist who went on to became a Labour MP and the party's deputy leader under Blair. Prescott was seen by some as the defender of pro-union positions. He had in fact produced an excellent defence of the 1966 seafarers' strike with a pamphlet called *Not Wanted on Voyage*. Yet, in 2002, the same Prescott, now deputy prime minister, denounced a strike by firefighters over pay as "completely unnecessary and unjustified" and claimed that it would undermine the ability of the government to go to war in Iraq since it would mean troops would have to be used to scab on firefighters (as indeed they were).

And this thread of hostility to strikes runs through every Labour government – including the 1945 Attlee government, held in the greatest esteem by Labour supporters thanks to its nationalisations and the creation of the NHS. Yet the same Attlee government while introducing such reforms also repeatedly sent troops in to scab on strikes. As one account put it:

> On 18 different occasions between 1945 and 1951, the government sent troops, sometimes 20,000 of them, across picket lines to take over strikers' jobs. By 1948, it has been argued, "strike-breaking had become almost second nature to the Cabinet".

Why has Labour repeatedly acted in this way? Labour's focus is on parliament and winning elections and forming a government. The assumption is that this is where real power lies in society, not workers' struggles. Labour seeks to work within capitalism and its institutions. But parliament has little power when it comes to challenging the interests of capitalism and the ruling class that presides over and benefits from it.

Any government seen as challenging the supremacy of profit or touching the privileges of the rich, is liable to quickly find that with its control over the economic levers of society, big business can apply huge pressure and force a retreat, or even break the government entirely. Even the modest reforms initially put forward by the Labour governments of 1964-70 and 1974-9 led to massive capital flight, forcing a currency crisis and investment strikes.

Such events are not simply a thing of history. This was also the fate of the Greek Syriza government, which was elected in 2015, on a similar type of programme to Corbyn's. Promising to reverse years of brutal austerity, it faced economic and financial blackmail to abandon this programme regardless of its democratic mandate. As the EU, IMF (International Monetary Fund) and Greek capital moved to force Alexis Tsipras's government to abandon its own manifesto, the then German finance minister, Wolfgang Schäuble, cynically but accurately expressed the ruling classes' real view of parliamentary democracy, "Elections cannot be allowed to change economic policy."

And if elected governments cannot be allowed to control the economic levers of society, nor do they control the state machine. Parliament is only a small island of democracy surrounded (and corrupted) by a vast ocean of powerful unelected hierarchies – the senior civil service, the judges, the police, the army, the intelligence services – that command the resources of the state.

Far from being neutral or subordinated to the wishes of democratically elected government, those who sit at the top of such hierarchies are tied to big business not just by shared class background, education and social networks. Even more fundamentally, they are tied by a mutual interest in sustaining and defending the profitability of British capitalism. They will subvert or block the implementation of policies and laws they see as a threat, spy and manoeuvre to weaken radical governments, and in a deep crisis use armed force to overthrow it.

Class and nation

As Tony Cliff and Donny Gluckstein note in their book *The Labour Party: A Marxist History*, the Labour Party was born as the "political expression of the trade union bureaucracy" – and it remains tied to the union bureaucracy through its numerous links to unions, even if that relationship is more diluted than in the past. Labour is a different political animal as a party than the Tories or the Liberals, which are openly ruling class parties with no links to workers' organisations.

But the trade union bureaucracy and the Labour Party play different roles.

> The Labour Party is purely electoral. Hence it relates to its supporters as a multitude of individuals. The trade union bureaucracy must relate to groups of workers as collectives. With this separation of politics and economics, the Labour Party leadership is always an outsider to industrial struggle. In contrast to this, the trade union bureaucracy can never completely avoid heading the industrial struggle, even if only in order to restrain it.

If the trade union bureaucracy is one step removed from the workplace, the Labour Party is two steps removed.

Labour is a combination of class and nation. It is an expression of working-class desire for reform within capitalism, but it also seeks to represent, and when in office to rule on behalf of, the nation. Yet under capitalism there is no common national interest that spans the divide of class exploitation. "Ruling for the nation" means defending the interests of capitalism and the ruling class. As a result, Labour in office ends up time and again imposing the imperatives of capitalism and standing in conflict with workers' struggles.

The Labour left and strikes

Labour is thus a contradiction – it contains within it two poles: open support for capitalism and an expression of workers' desire for reforms within capitalism. If Starmer, like Blair, is on the most reactionary side of this contradiction, then the Labour left embraces the other side, the desire for real change. So, Jeremy Corbyn has spent a lifetime as a Labour member, MP and party leader, identifying with strikes, opposing war and campaigning for justice.

But as the example of Syriza shows, if the Labour left were elected to form a government, it would face the same extreme pressures to abandon any promises for real change and impose attacks on workers or face being broken. But even in opposition, the Labour left's more sympathetic approach to workers' struggles has major limits.

One is that the Labour left is much more reluctant to back strikes that challenge Labour councils. The long strike by the Coventry refuse workers in 2022 was an embarrassment to the Labour left on the whole.

But secondly and ultimately most seriously, the Labour left also accepts the separation of politics and economics and sees its role as supporting strikes while leaving the actual strike leadership in the hands of the trade union bureaucracy. They do not see their role as contesting the strategy of the bureaucracy when it falls short of what is needed, nor do they see their role as organising their supporters within a union independently of the bureaucracy in order to fight for an approach best able to take a dispute to victory. This, however, is the task that revolutionaries must set for themselves.

Socialists and class politics in the workplace

The great lesson of the last year of strikes is that in the major national strikes the scale of confrontation with employers and government to win clear victories is much greater than the union bureaucracy has been willing to contemplate. The path to achieving the necessary scale of confrontation lies therefore in mounting a much greater challenge to the bureaucracy's leadership.

So, revolutionary socialists insist on the need to contest the strategy in disputes and to fight for the leadership of struggles. This means rejecting any separation of politics and economics, and seeking to unite them both in the workplace and link them to workers' struggles and organisation. Uniting politics and economics strengthens workers' capacity to fight.

What follows from this is that revolutionary socialists must aim to develop, over time, a culture of participation and involvement in workplace and trade union organisation. The model is not individual negotiating with managers, or simply focusing on individual case work, but developing a regular culture of meetings in a workplace and of collective challenges to management over grievances.

It means a democratic culture of debate and votes and acting on majority decisions. This means not abstaining from arguments, and it means trying to win people to positions even when in a minority. A socialist cannot just passively reflect the mood and views of their workplace, but has to attempt, over time through discussion and experience, to win a majority to a position, or to a course of action.

It also means resisting pressure not to raise criticisms or challenges to the union leadership and bureaucracy in the name of preserving unity. A failed strategy from the bureaucracy and, even worse, reps and activists being identified with such a strategy because they keep their own doubts and criticism quiet is a disaster and is precisely what creates division and demoralisation.

Raising support and solidarity for workers' struggles in other workplaces – taking a collection for a group of strikers, visiting their picket line, inviting a striker from a dispute to speak at a union meeting – all increase the sense of being part of a wider working-class movement and of learning from the struggles of other workers.

But the need to unite economics and politics means going beyond even this militant trade union approach. It involves raising political discussion and initiatives in the workplace, particularly the important aspect of challenging all forms of oppression. Taking up the defence of refugees at work in the face of racist demonisation by the government and media, passing a motion defending abortion rights or organising to send a banner to a Trans Pride event, and a myriad of other examples, far from being irrelevant to trade unionism, serve to strengthen workers' unity.

Taking up issues such as the urgent threat of climate change, building opposition to war and imperialism, raising solidarity with Palestine and with international workers' struggles and revolts, not only strengthen such struggles by rooting them in workers' organisation and power, but also broaden working-class consciousness by locating their own battles within a wider canvas.

Doing so develops workplace organisation in another way. It can help draw a new generation of activists, those influenced by mass movements over these questions, into building the union by helping them see that organising at work is a vital aspect of such fights. A union indifferent to these wider questions – from climate change to anti-racism or war –will find it much harder to bring in these new activists.

All these aspects of building effectively in the workplace need to be brought together in a total vision of social transformation and given organisational form. This means building socialist organisation inside, not just external to, the workplace – where socialists openly identify themselves at work, seek to win people to their politics and draw them towards engagement with socialist organisation. It means using socialist publications such as *Socialist Worker* in both physical and online forms at work to identify and influence those interested in such ideas and to create an organised network in the workplace and the union.

An Activist's Guide to Strikes and Trade Unions
First published in *Socialist Worker*

As the level of strikes began to rise in 2022, it soon became clear that many new activists were being drawn into the movement. Although enthused by workers' action, because of years of low levels of struggle they were unfamiliar with many of the basics of trade union organisation and the vocabulary of the workers' movement.

Socialist Worker ran a series of articles explaining these basic concepts which we reproduce here as a useful reference for readers of this book.

What's a picket line?
Picket lines – groups of strikers gathering outside their workplace – are the physical manifestation of strikes. They are there to stop workers from weakening the collective power of the action by going into work.

They can also turn away deliveries to the firm that's targeted. Those who cross the picket line – siding with the bosses and hurting their fellow-workers – are known as scabs. The word became widely used after socialist author Jack London wrote his "Ode to a Scab" in 1913.

A scab, said London, is "a two-legged animal with a corkscrew soul and a combination backbone made of jelly and glue. Where others have hearts, he carries a tumour of rotten principles."

A picket line shouldn't be a place of polite conversation where pleasantries are exchanged before someone goes into work. It's a site of persuasion, education and argument – but also confrontation.

Some of the key moments in British working-class history have involved mass pickets that physically blocked a workplace. That happened, for example, at Saltley Gate in 1972, a crucial moment during the successful miners' strike. Saltley was a fuel plant in Birmingham, where up to 700 vehicles were collecting fuel each day to supply industries. Mass pickets and walkouts in other factories saw 15,000 pickets close the plant and it became a symbol of militancy and effective action.

Pickets are also a vital organising hub for strikers. They are natural places to discuss the next steps for the strike and a sensible place to receive solidarity from socialists or trade unionists.

There's a reason why the Tories have imposed extra conditions on picket lines – such as formally limiting their size. Join picket lines, support picket lines. Never cross a picket line.

What are the anti-union laws?

British governments have passed laws outlawing or limiting trade unions for more than 200 years. Labour governments, as well as Tory ones, were frightened of union power and tried to weaken activists' organisation and tame union power.

Sometimes workers have fought back by mass strikes and made the laws impossible to implement. At other times they have organised politically to have the laws repealed.

Anti-union laws are pro-boss weapons in the class struggle. Each anti-union law makes it harder to take action. The threat is that a union could be sued if it doesn't follow the law.

Thatcher led the charge against organised workers with anti-union laws in the 1980s. These took strike decisions away from mass meetings and enforced individual postal ballots.

Unions lost control of their rule books and had to follow government dictates about internal elections. Solidarity action with other workers was outlawed.

And further laws in the 1990s meant all strike ballots had to be postal and unions had to give bosses notice of an intention to ballot.

The Trade Union Act in 2016 was a vicious attack on the right to strike. Critically, it brought in a minimum turnout threshold of

50 percent of members for strike ballots. And it imposed 14 days' notice period for walkouts.

The effect is obvious – the Tories want to make it harder for workers to strike, and to stall action when unions feel they have the wind behind them.

But none of these could have been implemented without union leaders accepting them.

And lots of union leaders liked the new laws because they gave them an excuse not to call action, and a way to discipline the more militant sections of the membership.

Now the Tories have pushed more anti-union laws. Activists have to push for them to be opposed. But, if they are passed, they also have to insist they are made inoperable through defiance.

What's rank-and-file organisation?
The main divide in every workplace is between workers and bosses. That leads to the creation of trade unions, which are important organisations and schools of struggle. But there's also a crucial division within unions between the ordinary union members and the full-time officials, the bureaucracy.

The bureaucracy is a mediating force between the union and the bosses. It does deals with the employers rather than seeing a battle through to the end by the most militant methods. That's because of their social role, not just because they are better paid and removed from the day-to-day pressures of the workplace.

The failures of the bureaucracy mean workers have sometimes organised networks of ordinary union members to pressure the officials and sometimes to act independently of them. This is what we mean by rank-and-file organisation. It is not an alternative to union membership, but a vital part of it. It's not creating a new union but fighting inside the existing one.

The Clyde Workers' Committee, formed by engineers in Glasgow, expressed the standpoint well during the First World War. "We will support the officials just so long as they rightly represent the workers, but we will act immediately they misrepresent them."

It organised strikes even when the bureaucracy refused to call them. And it also supported a rent strike of 25,000 tenants by threatening a general strike. Rank-and-file organisation depends on a network of union activists with real roots in their workplaces, able to pose the question of practical independent action among their members.

It is different from "Broad Lefts" in focusing on collective action, and not just union elections and conference policies.

What are strike committees?
The greater the participation by strikers in their own dispute, the better the chances of winning. Socialists argue for workers' democratic control of strikes. One way of organising this is by electing a strike committee to co-ordinate action and guide the fight to victory.

Union officials will claim that they fill this role. But while some of these may earn the right to be on the committee, others can be out of touch with the day-to-day mood and concerns of the workers. The role of a striker should not be reduced to voting for action and then passively watching events unfold until they are told to go back to work.

Picket lines are also a chance for workers to discuss the way forward. They have to be followed up by regular mass meetings, which can vote on proposals about how to win and the tactics of the dispute. They can also deal with people's inevitable worries and hesitations.

An elected committee can allow workers with ideas and experience to control the strike and battle bosses democratically and efficiently. In 2022-3 there were strike committees in some education strikes and in the North Sea unofficial action.

What is the TUC?
The Trades Union Congress (TUC) is the federation of trade unions. It brings together 48 unions with a total of 5.5 million members across England and Wales. There is also a separate but linked Scottish TUC.

At one time the TUC was seen as the "general staff" of the labour movement, orchestrating the strategy of the unions and welcomed as a negotiating partner by governments as a way of dampening down militancy.

Today individual unions, particularly the big unions, are the key decision-makers and the TUC is less powerful. But it can be important.

It co-ordinated the big demonstration in June 2022 that saw tens of thousands on the "Britain Demands Better" protest in London.

The TUC is even further removed from workers than the leaders of the individual unions. It doesn't directly have any members who can hold it to account. When workers strike, they think of what their own union leaders are saying and doing, not so much the TUC.

The general council, the leadership body of the TUC, is made up of the top layer of the union bureaucracy. So the decisions it makes reflect the interests of that narrow group.

High office in the TUC is often a route to mainstream acceptance. Baroness Frances O'Grady received a life peerage in October 2022 as she was retiring as TUC leader.

Her predecessor Sir Brendan Barber was knighted for "services to employment relations".

At key moments, when it seems like the working class is on the front foot, the TUC has played a decisive role in negotiating peace – or surrender – with the bosses.

A good example is the 1926 General Strike, when the TUC called off the action and negotiated a rotten deal with the government just as the strike was expanding and raising issues of revolution.

Are the unions democratic?
Everyone should be a member of a union in their workplace and should be an active trade unionist.

It is a crucial forum for organising collectively against employers, and a great way to raise class conscious politics.

Different unions have different rules but each one is more democratic than the Tories and big corporations. Formally, unions have a big apparatus that enables layers of democracy. Union members can elect the general secretary and the leadership bodies. These votes matter.

But even when militants secure such positions there are then immense pressures to draw them into the bureaucratic world cut off from those who elected them. Even in the most democratic union, full-time officials can call off strikes – for instance, to consider a bad deal – even before workers are consulted.

The key democratic bodies should be mass meetings of union members and strikers, elected committees of strikers during disputes, and meetings of union reps within a firm, industry or service and across different workplaces.

These can put pressure on the officials, or organise independently of them. Join a union, be active and raise wider politics as well as battles in the workplace.

What is an indefinite strike?

All strikes matter. They point to the difference between bosses and the people they exploit. But there is a big difference between a carefully-controlled one-day strike and one that sets out to continue until victory is achieved.

An indefinite strike is one that isn't time limited. It goes on until a deal is agreed by the strikers. There were some very effective examples of indefinite strikes among bus workers in 2022-3, and they generally won better settlements than those who took intermittent strikes.

Often they can secure a win quicker than a series of one-day or two-day strikes. During an indefinite strike it's much easier for workers to organise to win solidarity from others, hold meetings, and take part in marches and rallies. There is also a greater chance of democracy from below.

A number of unions held 18 or more days of strikes in 2022-3, but spread out over many months. If an indefinite strike had extended over so long a period, it would almost certainly have seen victory. But a spread-out strike can often be ineffective.

You will also hear the phrase "all out" strikes. Sometimes this is just another way of saying indefinite strikes. But it can also be a call for everyone in a workplace, industry or union to strike together for a set amount of time.

A radical conclusion of uniting workers' strikes is a "general strike" – a walkout by millions of workers across industries. Workers in Britain are capable of a general strike. The TUC union federation in 2011 co-ordinated ballots that saw 2.5 million public sector workers strike together for one day over pension attacks.

It wasn't a general strike, but it pointed the way towards the potential for one. In the 1926 British General Strike, millions of workers struck for nine days. They were then sent back to work by their union leaders without any gains.

After 12 weeks on strike, workers lose some special legal protections. And after six months the anti-union laws demand a new ballot to continue a strike. So when there are intermittent strikes these factors can be used to strangle action.

What are co-ordinated strikes?

Co-ordinated strikes mean that people strike on the same day across industries and unions. This happened on 1 February and 15 March 2023 when hundreds of thousands struck. This enabled big demonstrations, and workers gaining confidence from each other's battles.

Such strikes make clear that companies and government ministers face a movement of the class, not just an individual set of strikers.

Sometimes union leaders and activists say they want to keep the media focus on their dispute by striking on different days. But the reality is that strikes are often ignored by the media.

A day when huge numbers of workers strike dominates the news agenda and means there's widespread discussion of the issues involved.

Another argument is that it's "more effective" for, say, one rail union to strike one day and the other unions another day because both sets of action close the network. It's important to think about the potency of action. But bosses aren't moved by "clever tactics".

Strikes have to create a crisis for the companies and for the Tories. Another important argument is that united action is a beacon for the whole working class.

Days of united action can be a focus for people not in unions and those not in work. It could win support from campaigns over poverty, benefits, the climate crisis, racism and more.

But some union leaders use the idea of co-ordinated action as a barrier to actually calling strikes. They say they will move only if other unions do as well. The message should be: "United if we can, on our own if we must".

Should workers fight for strike pay?

In most types of strikes, workers in most unions are entitled to a daily rate of strike pay, typically set at a rate lower than they'd usually earn. Unions like to boast of their million-pound "war chests" as part of sabre-rattling ahead of key disputes.

They do this to scare the bosses and reassure members that they can afford to stay out long enough to win. Strikers should fight to receive proper support from their unions, so people aren't forced to give up action prematurely. After all, it is funded through their membership fees.

For instance, it was a good development when the industrial action committee at the Unison union doubled daily strike pay from £25 to £50 a day.

But strike pay is double-edged. If workers believe they can't strike without it, then it means if the union officials stop paying up, then the strike ends.

It becomes a weapon of control for them. Activists should never argue that walkouts can only happen if there is sufficient strike pay to cushion workers from any hardship. The reality is that striking often involves short-term financial loss, but a victory results in better deals and stronger organisation.

Extended strikes mean workers have to cope with a much-reduced pay packet. Raising money for strikers is important. It funds people on the picket lines, and also raises the political profile of the strike in general.

And it's also very important for those who do a collection among their fellow workers. It means the message of strikes is spread more widely, and activists can see who gives to the collection. These are people who can be won to struggle in the future.

By appealing to other workers for financial solidarity, strikers put an important argument that the success of their own dispute will make it easier for other workers to win.

One good example is the National Gallery dispute of 2015. Workers won a long-running all-out strike, partly through how successfully they won solidarity in the wider trade union movement. Despite not being paid their full wages by their PCS union, they could resist bosses' pressure for them to end the strike.

This was partly achieved by strikers speaking at trade union meetings and showing up to picket lines for other workers in dispute. It's a good example that shows the success of a dispute can't simply boil down to how well unions fund strike pay.

What should non-unionised workers do?

Socialists think all workers should join a trade union in their workplace. But not being a member of a union isn't a block to taking some action. Whatever workplace you are in, it is possible to start organising for better pay, against bullying bosses and for better conditions.

The first step has to be talking to your colleagues, working out who shares your grievances and wants to fight back. The next could be pulling those people into a group that can discuss what to do next. Often you can start with issues outside the immediate workplace – anger about racism or action over climate chaos for example.

Bringing workers together to sign a letter or a petition can make it clear that workers have demands and that they will fight collectively until they are met. When workers start to realise their strength, the next step could be to organise a "wildcat strike". These kinds of strikes do not go through the processes of organising postal ballots and all the other obstacles outlined in the Tory anti-union laws.

An inspiring wave of resistance through Amazon facilities in the summer of 2022 showed it's possible to resist without a union. Workers engaged in walkouts and slowdowns to stop the job "becoming a rapid descent into hell", one striker told *Socialist Worker*. And the Coventry warehouse is an excellent example about how wildcat action can lead to longer-term organisation.

Some workers there joined the GMB union and launched official strikes in 2023. This then led to workers at other sites joining the union and balloting for action.

Union officials are keen to recruit workers who organise wildcat strikes, not just because it will swell their membership numbers or because they'll win. Some want to maintain a degree of control over the momentum of the labour movement in general.

That shouldn't put workers off joining unions where possible. But it is right to be wary about the kind of role the crushing weight of formal processes may play in their action.

What is solidarity?
Solidarity is the idea that those fighting should not fight alone – but it's more than just a feeling of unity. Solidarity could mean respecting a picket line and not crossing it or sending a message of support.

It could also mean making a financial donation to a strike fund or bringing along sandwiches to strikers. Raising solidarity isn't just about asking for practical support for the dispute but about winning the argument that everyone in the working class benefits when fightbacks win.

Solidarity can take many forms, but the most effective is workers taking action together. It's this type of working-class unity that the ruling class hate – that's why, officially, solidarity strikes are illegal under the anti-Tory laws.

But that wouldn't stop workers – engaged in official disputes in their workplaces – striking simultaneously and hitting the bosses hard.

Winning the argument about delivering solidarity means wider numbers of people will get involved when there is resistance.

If a delegation of students supports a picket line, they'll know which union rep to contact next time they go into occupation and are calling out for a helping hand themselves. Ultimately solidarity is about more than supporting individual disputes. It's about building links between different groups of people, making the entire working-class movement stronger as a result.

Hasn't the working class changed too much?

After some crushing defeats for working-class people in the 1980s, paving the way for the onslaught of free market attacks on jobs and services, there's been no shortage of such arguments. They're rooted in changes that do seem to have taken place. The supposed decline of the manufacturing industry for instance, and the apparent rise of jobs in the service, IT or financial sectors.

These are jobs that maybe couldn't have been dreamed of in the 1920s or 1970s, when the working class was at the height of its power.

And, some arguments suggest, they mean workers can no longer use their power in the way they once did. Work now is precarious, we are told. It's unorganised and concentrated in jobs that don't have the same importance to profit-making.

It's true the working class is changing – and always has. Capitalism means firms and industries constantly find new ways to make profits.

Whole industries rise while others fall into the dust. New jobs are created and others are smashed. And bosses are always looking for new ways to squeeze us.

They want new ways to make us work harder for less, new ways to monitor and measure us, and new ways to keep us apart. Jobs that we might think of as citadels of union power in the past – such as dockers – were once also considered too precarious or unorganised to fight.

Sometimes, though, the scale or impact of these changes can be exaggerated. For instance, the number of people in temporary jobs in Britain made up just 6 percent of the workforce in 2021. And far from being fragmented, about half of private sector workers in Britain are employed by companies with 100 or more workers. The vast majority of these work for companies with 500 or more. That gives them considerable potential power.

Capitalism, whatever way it is organised, is compelled to push us together to exploit us for profit. That means two things. First, it means firms and industries depend on our labour to make those profits, whether we're manufacturing goods, distributing them or selling them on. We're all united by that shared exploitation giving us the collective strength to disrupt or shut them down.

Secondly, because production is organised across society, small groups of workers can have a big impact. People at one point of the production chain depend on others. Relatively small groups can shut down entire networks.

Amazon is often held up as the prime example of the powerlessness of workers in "new" industries. But thousands of people are drawn together into its warehouses, the nodes of its distribution and delivery networks. If they strike, they cause disruption far beyond their own workplace.

What's more, capitalism also has to create a web of other jobs, all designed to facilitate production. Industries and firms all need caterers, cleaners, call centre agents, IT technicians and many more to function.

They need teachers to provide a skilled workforce. They need train and bus drivers to get them to work. And they need shop assistants so that workers are clothed and fed.

Everyone is tied into the system in some way or other. So we're powerful, even if we don't necessarily feel that we are. It's a question of confidence and organisation.

Both of those took a battering after the defeats of the 1980s. All too often since, union leaders used those defeats to argue that fighting was no longer possible. This current wave of strikes is an opportunity to prove that wrong – and in the process rebuild organisation in every workplace and industry.

Further Reading

The SWP's quarterly journal, *International Socialism*, has some useful articles about the strike wave that began in 2022. It is available both in book form and online (www.isj.org.uk). See, for example, Mark L Thomas, "Striking back: is the class struggle reviving in Britain?", *International Socialism* 176 (2022), Charlie Kimber, "Britain's strike wave: workers on the frontline", *International Socialism* 177 (2023) and Joseph Choonara, "The British labour movement's halting recovery", *International Socialism* 178 (2023).

A vital source of reports, information and analysis of developments in the strikes is *Socialist Worker* (www.socialistworker.co.uk/socialist-worker/).

The classic Marxist analysis of the trade union bureaucracy can be found in Tony Cliff and Donny Gluckstein, *Marxism and the Trade Union Struggle: The General Strike of 1926* (Bookmarks, 1986). This also covers developments in the class struggle from 1910 through to the defeat of the general strike in 1926.

Alex Callinicos's 1982 article, "The rank-and-file movement today" in *International Socialism* 17, gives a good restatement of the theory of the bureaucracy but also provides a useful overview of the rise and fall of rank-and-file movements up to the late 1970s. It is available online at: www.marxists.org/history/etol/writers/callinicos/1982/xx/rfmvmt.html

James Hinton's classic study, *The First Shop Stewards' Movement* (1973), details the emergence of the Clyde Workers' Committee and the shop stewards' movement in the First World War. It's long out of print but well worth getting hold of a second hand copy if you can.

And Chris Harman's article, "1984 and the shape of things to come" in *International Socialism* 29 (1985) provides a detailed but valuable survey and analysis of the period from the long post-war boom, the upturn of workers' militancy in the early 1970s and its containment and then defeats under the Labour and then Thatcher governments from the mid-1970s onwards. It can be found online at: www.marxists.org/archive/harman/1985/xx/miners.html